CULTURE SMART!
AZERBAIJAN

Nikki Kazimova

·K·U·P·E·R·A·R·D·

ISBN 978 1 85733 544 6
This book is also available as an e-book: eISBN 978 1 85733 548 4

British Library Cataloguing in Publication Data
A CIP catalogue entry for this book is available from the British Library

First published in Great Britain 2011
by Kuperard, an imprint of Bravo Ltd
59 Hutton Grove, London N12 8DS
Tel: +44 (0) 20 8446 2440 Fax: +44 (0) 20 8446 2441
www.culturesmart.co.uk
Inquiries: sales@kuperard.co.uk

Distributed in the United States and Canada
by Random House Distribution Services
1745 Broadway, New York, NY 10019
Tel: +1 (212) 572-2844 Fax: +1 (212) 572-4961
Inquiries: csorders@randomhouse.com

Series Editor Geoffrey Chesler
Design Bobby Birchall

Printed in Malaysia

contents

contents

About the Author

NIKKI KAZIMOVA is a Baku-born cross-cultural trainer and freelance writer. An honors graduate from the Azerbaijan University of Culture and Arts, she has an MA in journalism from the University of Missouri-Columbia.

Over the last ten years, Nikki has been dividing her time between Azerbaijan and the USA, where she studied and worked in journalism and for media development organizations, including CNN International and the International Center for Journalists in Washington.

She has worked for ExxonMobil in Azerbaijan, was a regional correspondent for Bloomberg News and the International Journalists Network, and was consultant to nonprofit organizations in Baku and Washington. She also managed the communication campaign of the Council of Europe's "All Different All Equal" program in Strasbourg. She was an adjunct lecturer at Khazar University in Baku, and has conducted training courses for young journalists.

The Culture Smart! series is continuing to expand.
For further information and latest titles visit
www.culturesmart.co.uk

The publishers would like to thank **CultureSmart!**Consulting for its help in researching and developing the concept for this series.

CultureSmart!Consulting creates tailor-made seminars and consultancy programs to meet a wide range of corporate, public-sector, and individual needs. Whether delivering courses on multicultural team building in the USA, preparing Chinese engineers for a posting in Europe, training call-center staff in India, or raising the awareness of police forces to the needs of diverse ethnic communities, it provides essential, practical, and powerful skills worldwide to an increasingly international workforce.

For details, visit www.culturesmartconsulting.com

CultureSmart!Consulting and **CultureSmart!** guides have both contributed to and featured regularly in the weekly travel program "Fast Track" on BBC World TV.

Map of Azerbaijan

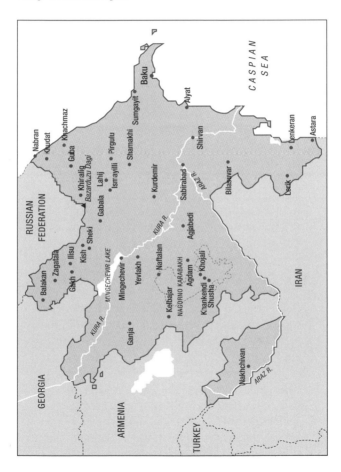

introduction

Azerbaijan, which has recently joined the global family as an independent state, is not an easy place to understand. It is a former Soviet republic with a complex identity that includes a linguistic kinship with Turkey, religious similarity with Shi'a Iran, and Russian cultural influences.

Strategically located between Russia, Iran, and Turkey, the country is rich in oil reserves, which means that it is inevitably involved in the new Great Game of our times. While trying to balance its relations with Russia, which still views the Caucasus as its own backyard, Azerbaijan has signed the "Contract of the Century" with major international oil companies to develop its Caspian Sea hydrocarbon reserves, and built pipelines to deliver oil and gas directly to European markets.

As oil rigs drill and the pumping gear pumps the "black gold" of Azerbaijan, the proliferation of black Land Cruiser Prados on the streets of Baku is testament to its transforming power; it took the country out of extreme poverty in the early 1990s and into the ranks of those countries applying to host the summer Olympics in 2016.

But, despite Azerbaijan's declared desire to belong to Europe and the wider Western world, make no mistake about its origins. If you are struck by the European architecture and women's liberal dress styles in the streets of Baku, remember that you are still in Asia. Geographically, Baku is closer to Kabul, Tehran, and Istanbul than to Moscow, from where it was managed on and off for nearly two centuries before independence in 1991.

The Azerbaijani people, divided by an arbitrary border drawn after the Russo-Persian wars in the early nineteenth century, number tens of millions, only a fraction of whom live in the Republic of Azerbaijan. The largest number live in northwestern Iran, and many are scattered around the globe.

Today the Azerbaijanis are pondering their complex heritage and trying to define their destiny. This book will acquaint you with the basics of their history and social norms. Reading about their notions of friendship, ways of raising children, and which topics of conversation to cover and which to avoid, you will find the process of navigating the unfamiliar cultural undertows much less daunting. With time, you'll be able to engage in conversations, form partnerships, and enjoy friendships that are likely to last a lifetime.

The genuine warmth and readiness to help that typify the Azerbaijani people will captivate you, and their poetic ways will beguile you. You may not always get a direct answer to your questions, and will often have to decipher the hidden meanings of verbal statements, but if you don't allow these subtleties to discourage you, you will find a people who are loyal, sensitive, and resourceful. Hospitality is one of the cornerstones of their society, and the phrase you are likely to hear most often in Azerbaijan is "*Khosh gelmisiniz!*"—"Welcome!"

Key Facts

Official Name	Republic of Azerbaijan (Azerbaijan Respublikasi)	On October 18, 1991, Azerbaijan declared its independence from the Soviet Union, confirmed by a referendum in December 1991.
Capital City	Baki	The international name is Baku.
Major Cities	Shirvan, Ganja, Khankendi, Lenkeran, Mingechevir, Naftalan, Sumgayit, Sheki, Shusha, Yevlakh	Khankendi and Shusha are currently in the occupied zone.
Area	33,436 sq. miles (86,600 sq. km)	
Borders	Land borders with Russia, Iran, Turkey, Georgia, and Armenia. Shares Caspian Sea borders with Kazakhstan, Turkmenistan, Iran, and Russia	
Climate	Semidesert around Baku; subtropical in the south; forest, alpine, and subalpine in the northwest; semi-desert and mountainous tundra in Nakhchivan	A total of 9 climatic zones
Currency	1 Azeri manat (AZN) = 100 gepik	In 2010, 1 manat was US$1.25, GBP 0.79, EUR 0.90.

Population	9 million (February 2010)	
Language	Azerbaijani. Russian still spoken in some circles	Alphabet changed 4 times throughout 20th century
Religion	93% Muslim. Majority are Shi'a	Other religions include Catholicism, Protestantism, Russian Orthodoxy, Buddhism, Bahaí, and Judaism.
Government	Republic with universal suffrage. President is the head of state, elected every 5 years. No limit on the number of consecutive presidential terms	The single-chamber parliament, the Milli Majlis, has 125 deputies, elected every 5 years. President appoints the prime minister, with the consent of the Milli Majlis
Media	AZTV channel is government-owned. ITV is public television funded by the state. Main private TV stations are Lider, ANS, ATV, Khazar, and Space.	Major print publications in the Azerbaijani language are *525 gazet*, *Azadliq*, *Yeni Musavat*; Russian-language *Echo*, *Zerkalo*, *Nedelya*.
Electricity	220 volts, 50 Hz	2-prong plugs
Video/TV	PAL/SECAM	DVD players will not play NTSC discs.
Internet Domain	.az	
Telephone	Country code is 994. Baku code is 12	To call out, dial 00 and country code.
Time Zone	GMT + 4	Daylight saving start/end dates are in late March and late October.

LAND &
PEOPLE

GEOGRAPHY

Azerbaijan is the biggest of the three countries in
the southern Caucasus, located on the southwestern
shore of the Caspian Sea. As a rather small state that
only made its way on to the contemporary world
map in 1991, it may be hard to pinpoint. Some
maps of Europe include Muslim Azerbaijan;
others leave it out. It has been classified as being
in "Europe," in "Asia," or in "the Middle East."

The country borders Russia and Georgia in the
north, Armenia and Turkey in the west, and Iran
in the south. The map of Azerbaijan resembles an
eagle, with its beak pointing to the capital, Baku,
on the Caspian peninsula.

The country's highest peak is Bazarduzu Dagi,
14,652 feet (4,466 m) tall in the Lesser Caucasus
Mountains and its lowest point is the Caspian
Sea, which lies 92 feet (28 m) below sea level.

The oil-rich Caspian Sea is bordered by five
states—Russia, Iran, Turkmenistan, Kazakhstan,
and Azerbaijan—that have not yet arrived at a joint
conclusion about its status. So far, Azerbaijan,
Russia, and Kazakhstan have reached an agreement
on the status of the Caspian, which has been
rejected by Iran and Turkmenistan.

Although Azerbaijan is landlocked, Baku has an international port from which passenger ferries sail off across the Caspian to Turkmenistan and Kazakhstan, and which also handles significant cargo traffic in petroleum products. Built in 1902, it is the largest Caspian port. Azerbaijan's two main rivers, the Kura and the Araz, flow into the Caspian.

The land near Baku is saturated with oil and gas, and a popular version of the origin of Azerbaijan's name is "The Land of Fire," from the Persian word *azer*, which means "fire."

The country's total area of 33,400 sq. miles (86,600 sq. km) includes the autonomous republic of Nakhchivan—the only part of Azerbaijan that shares a short, 5.6 mile (9 km) border with Turkey—which is separated from the rest of Azerbaijan by a narrow strip of Armenia. It also includes a region called Daglig (Mountainous) Garabag in Azeri, or Nagorno Karabakh in Russian, which has been occupied by Armenian forces since the early 1990s, together with the surrounding villages.

CLIMATE

From the dry sands of Baku to the lush hills of the Caucasus Mountains, Azerbaijan has a variety of climate types and Azerbaijanis like to boast that their small land has nine of the climate zones described in the Köppen-Geiger classification system.

In Baku, summers are long and hot, with average temperatures around 86°F (30°C). Winters are cold and windy, with temperatures rarely falling much below 32°F (0°C) but they feel much colder because of the strong winds. Autumns are mild, and springs are short. On average, the city gets one or two snowfalls in the winter, which cause havoc on its roads and streets, but the snow piles usually melt in just a few days.

Baku, which has an average of more than 300 sunny days a year, is also called the City of Winds,

 and lives up to this name most days of the year. The sunny and dry parts of Azerbaijan were used throughout the Soviet years for growing cotton, and they also lend themselves well to the cultivation of grapes, tomatoes, cucumbers, potatoes, and other vegetables.

The densely forested areas in the north, south, and west of the country have climates conducive to growing a variety of fruits and nuts, as well as

tobacco, silk, and subtropical citrus fruits. The western areas currently under Armenian occupation are hilly, green, and rich in mineral resources, including copper and gold.

The oil-producing land around Baku is arid and most trees in the Windy City were planted manually within the past 200 years. In his 1902 account of Baku, the British traveler Arnold Henry Savage Landor wrote, "The most depressing sight in Baku is the vegetation. The terrific heat of Baku, the hot winds and sand-storms are deadly enemies to vegetation. Nothing will grow. One does not see a blade of grass nor a shrub anywhere except those few that are artificially brought up. The sand is most trying. It is so fine that the wind forces it through anything, and one's tables, one's chairs, one's bed are yellow-coated with it . . . ."

Water shortage is a perennial problem. In 1900 the *New York Times* reprinted this excerpt from the engineering monthly *Cassier's Magazine* about Baku: "The water used by this city of over 75,000 inhabitants is now either distilled from the sea water, brought in tank cars from the distant rivers, or borne in casks on the backs of horses or camels from very carefully preserved wells in the vicinity and fed by not too frequent rains."

THE AZERBAIJANI PEOPLE

Azerbaijan's population, as of early 2010, was 9 million. The birth of the 9 millionth citizen was widely publicized in the local media and he received an equivalent of US$25,000 in local currency and an apartment in Baku from the president.

The population is young—every third Azerbaijani citizen is a person between fourteen and twenty-nine years of age (more than 60 percent of the total population is younger than twenty-nine). Life expectancy is sixty-three years for men, and seventy-one for women.

The boy-to-girl birth ratio is slowly tipping in the direction of more boys and fewer girls born every year, a trend, experts say, that is influenced by late-term abortions performed after ultrasound results reveal the fetus to be female.

There are also an estimated 20 million Azeris living in neighboring Iran, although their exact number is disputed between Azeri activists, who inflate it to 25 to 30 million, and Iranian official sources, which say that, according to the latest census, there are no more than 10 million living in the four traditionally Azerbaijani provinces—Eastern and Western Azerbaijan, Ardabil, and Zanjan.

Ethnic Minorities

According to the official statistics, about 90 percent of Azerbaijani citizens identify themselves as ethnic Azerbaijanis. The remaining 10 percent include Lezghins, Talysh, Russians, Armenians, Avars, Metskhetian Turks, Tatars, Kurds, Tats, and many others. Various sources mention up to eighty minorities scattered around small villages throughout Azerbaijan. They include hundreds of thousands of Lezghins, 76,000 Talysh in the north and south, and about 4,000 Udins, descendants of the ancient Caucasian Albanians.

Azerbaijanis are proud of the fact that their country has historically been free of anti-Semitism. There are two distinct Jewish communities in Azerbaijan, called the "European" and the "Mountain" Jews.

A BRIEF HISTORY

The historian Tadeusz Swietochowski calls Azerbaijan "the quintessential borderland, many times over: between Europe and Asia, Islam and Christianity, Russia and the Middle East, Turks and Iranians, Shi'a and Sunni Islam."

Azerbaijanis trace their ethnic roots to the Oghuz Turkic tribes, who swept across the Central Asian steppes in the eleventh century. However, unlike the neighboring Turks, who are Sunni Muslims, the Azeris are Shia, having been converted in the sixteenth century by the Safavid dynasty.

The country's most recent history (the past two hundred years) is connected with Russia, which annexed the territory of present-day Azerbaijan from Persia in the early nineteenth century, dividing the Azerbaijani people who lived on both sides of the new border along the Araz River. Most of them remained south of the Araz, in modern-day Iran, where Azerbaijanis are the biggest ethnic minority, concentrated primarily in the north of the country, with a regional center in the city of Tabriz.

The *Encyclopædia Britannica* describes the area of Iranian Azerbaijan as a "geographic region that comprises the extreme northwestern portion of Iran . . . bounded on the east by the Iranian region of Gilan and the Caspian Sea; on the south by the Iranian regions of Zanjan and Kordestan; and on the west by Iraq and Turkey . . . about 40,000 square miles [100,000 sq. km] in area."

The territory of Azerbaijan lay on the route of the Great Silk Road, an ancient network of trade paths that connected China with Europe, and its people have lived through centuries of conquests by different imperial powers. It is also situated in the heart of the Great Game, the struggle for control of Central Asia played out between Russia and the West at the turn on the nineteenth century, which seems to be going through a modern remake. Azerbaijan, like the rest of the Caucasus countries, has to balance its relations with the greater powers vying for economic and political control of its territory.

Antiquity and Medieval History
The lands south of the Araz (in the parts of Iran where ethnic Azeris live today) were part of the

ancient state of Mannea and then of the Medes (or Madai) from the tenth through the fifth centuries BCE.

In the fourth century BCE, the territory was conquered by Alexander the Great in battles with the Persian king Darius III, the last monarch of the Persian Achaemenid Empire. A local *satrap* (governor) under the name of Atropat (Aderbatag) negotiated autonomous ruling privileges for his province and eventually, after Alexander's death, it became an independent state under the name of Atropatene or Aderbatgan, which with time transformed into Azerbaijan. The population of the area practiced the Zoroastrian religion.

When Rome clashed with the Parthians in the first century BCE, Atropatene allied with Parthia and eventually became one of its provinces, in the year 20 BCE.

Much of the present-day Azerbaijan's territory, lying north of the Araz, was part of a different state. After the collapse of the Achaemenid Empire in the late fourth to early third centuries BCE, Albanian tribes living in what is now the Republic of Azerbaijan formed a new state called Caucasian Albania (not to be confused with the modern country of Albania in southeast Europe). Oghuz Turkic tribes, who arrived here soon after and mixed with the local population, called this land Arran.

Arran was conquered by the Romans in the first century CE and then by the Persian Sassanid Empire in the third century. By the fourth

century, its population had adopted Christianity
as the state religion.

Introduction of Islam
In the seventh and eighth centuries,
Arab invaders swept through the region
and converted the populations living
north and south of the Araz to Islam,
forcing out both Christianity and Zoroastrianism.

Early Shirvanshahs
By the ninth century, however, the Arab Caliphate
was weakening. The lands under the name of
Shirvan, which lay in the eastern part of Arran,
came under control of the new rulers called the
Shirvanshahs, who would remain the sovereign
monarchs of Shirvan for centuries.

Turkic Influence
Meanwhile, the Oghuz Turkic tribes were settling
in the territory of the Caucasus and northern Iran
and created the Seljuk Empire in the eleventh
century, a process that laid the foundation for the
formation of Azeri ethnicity.

Another hundred years later, as the Seljuk
Empire was declining, some of its territories were
ruled by the officers of the Kipchak tribe under the
name of Atabegs. In 1174, the city of Tabriz became
the capital of this large thriving state, until it
fell prey to a Mongol invasion in 1225 and
remained under their control for two centuries.

Azerbaijanis consider the eleventh and twelfth
centuries to be a golden age in their history.

The period gave birth to such notable figures of Azerbaijani culture as the poet Nizami Ganjavi, the scholar Khatib Tebrizi, the architect Ajami, and many others.

In 1410, the territory south of the Araz became part of the Kara Koyunlu (Black Sheep Turkomans) state with its capital in Tabriz, in present-day Iran. At that time, northern Azerbaijan was still ruled by the Shirvanshahs.

In the middle of the fifteenth century, Tabriz became the capital of the new powerful state of Ak Koyunlu (White Sheep Turkomans). The founder

of the dynasty, Uzun Hassan, waged war with the emergent Ottoman Turkey. He composed the *Ganunname*, a code of laws, and commissioned the translation of the Koran into Azeri. After his death, the Ak Koyunlu state split into two parts and ceased to exist.

According to some scholars, the most important Azerbaijani heroic epic, *Kitabi Dede Gorgud* (*The Book of Dede Korkut*), was written at around that time, though earlier versions of this narrative had been part of the oral tradition of the nomadic Oghuz tribes for centuries.

Shirvanshahs

Meanwhile, in the fifteenth century the state of the Shirvanshahs was thriving. It was famous for its exports of silk and gave rise to a material and intellectual culture that was highly respected in its time and whose creators are major figures in the

history of Azerbaijan. Among them was a poet named Nasimi, who wrote his *ghazels* (poems) in the Azeri language, unlike his predecessors who wrote in Persian and Arabic. The fifteenth-century Shirvanshahs' Palace is one of the landmarks of Baku's historic Old City.

Safavid Dynasty

In the early 1500s, the Shirvanshah state was forced to capitulate to the army of the Persian Savafid dynasty, which consolidated power over a vast territory in Asia, with a capital in Tabriz. The original Safavid dynasty were the Qizilbash, an ethnic Turkic (Azeri) tribe whose members demonstrated their devotion to Shi'a belief by wearing twelve red stripes on their turbans to commemorate the twelve imams revered in the Shi'a tradition.

Shah Ismail I, who ruled the Safavid state from 1501, unified the entire territory of present-day Iran. His reign was marked by the elevation of the status of Azeri to the official language of the royal court. Shah Ismail also wrote poetry in Azeri under the pen name of Khatai.

Another prominent writer who promoted the Azerbaijani literary tradition was Muhammad Bin Suleyman, known by the pen name Fuzuli. Science and the arts also thrived throughout the following century, producing such treasures as one of the largest libraries in the region in Tabriz, exquisite miniature paintings, and beautiful carpets.

The Safavid dynasty made Shi'a Islam the official religion of the state, although some Azeris remained Sunni.

At the end of the sixteenth century, Ottoman Turkey's attacks on the Safavid territories became more frequent and they conquered several provinces. The Iranian Shah Abbas I, who ruled the Safavid territory at the time, started drastic army reforms and eliminated many of the Turkic Qizilbash emirs before waging a war against the Ottomans and recapturing the provinces.

Independent Khanates

After the decline of the Safavids, the territory, although still nominally under Persian sovereignty, broke up into independently ruled provinces, or khanates.

Throughout the eighteenth century, Azerbaijan was torn by internal fighting between the khanates—mainly the Guba Khanate, the Sheki Khanate, the Karabakh Khanate, the Talysh Khanate, the Baku Khanate, the Ganja Khanate, the Nakhchivan Khanate, the Shirvan Khanate, the Derbent Khanate, and the Irevan Khanate.

A powerful khan of Sheki named Haji Chelebi fought and declared Sheki an independent khanate, which existed until Chelebi died in 1755. After his death, the Sheki Khanate lost its former might. Then, between 1758 and 1789, Fath-Ali Khan of Guba unified most of the khanates under his power, but after his death the wars continued.

In 1805, the Azerbaijani Karabakh khan Ibrahim Halil signed a treaty with Russia that made the Karabakh Khanate a Russian protectorate. After that, some Azeri Muslim families moved from their homes in Karabakh to Persia, while the Russian government encouraged Armenians living in Persia to move to Karabakh.

Russian Invasion and Russo-Persian Wars

In 1722, the Russian Czar Peter the Great brought his troops to the Caspian port of Astrakhan, from where they sailed off to Baku. After heavy shelling of the city walls by the Russian artillery, in 1723 Baku fell.

At the end of the eighteenth century, the Iranian throne was taken by the Qajar dynasty, which reasserted its rule over Azerbaijan and reincorporated most of the khanates into Iranian territory. However, Russia soon took back many of the lost provinces. The Russian general Pavel Tsitsianov, who had led the siege of Baku, was assassinated near the city gate in February 1806. Six months later, Russian forces fully occupied Baku and its last khan, Husseyn Gulu, fled into exile.

During the Russo-Persian war of 1804–13, Russia conquered a part of Azerbaijan and in 1813 signed the Treaty of Gulistan with Persia, according to which the territories of all the khanates north of the Araz River were transferred to Russian control. Some Muslim landowners were granted Russian nobility status.

About the Treaty of Gulistan, which "ratified the status quo resulting from the Russian military presence," Swietochowski writes: "The shah's claims to the northern Azerbaijani khanates were dismissed on the grounds that they had been independent long before their occupation by Russia. This amounted to the first and only recognition of Azerbaijani independence, albeit in the past sense."

In 1828, after two more years of war, Persia signed another peace agreement with the advancing Russians, called the Treaty of Turkmenchay, which made the final transfer of the Irevan, Nakhchivan, and the remainder of the Talysh Khanates to Russian control. This treaty completed the division of the Azerbaijanis living north and south of the Araz River. While they at that time were defined as "Turki" in Iran, the Russians called them "Aderbeijani Tartars."

"Oil Boom"

After Azerbaijan became a part of the Russian Empire, its provinces, previously called khanates, became Russian gubernias, and Baku was included in the newly created Shemakha Gubernia. In 1859, after an earthquake leveled the city of Shemakha, the gubernia's center was transferred to Baku.

This coincided with the start of commercial development of oil in Baku. In 1848 the first oil well in the world was drilled in Bibi Eybat near Baku, which was soon followed by the Azerbaijani equivalent of the Gold Rush. In 1872, the czarist government allowed the oil-producing land to be auctioned off to private companies, and businessmen from around the world flocked to Baku to make their fortunes. The most famous individuals to make handsome profits from the sale of Baku oil were the Rothschilds and the Nobel brothers. The first oil tankers sailed off the Caspian coast between 1880 and 1885, and the Baku–Batumi pipeline was built from 1897 to 1907. By the beginning of the twentieth century, half of the world's oil production was located in Baku.

During the "oil boom," Baku entered a phase of rapid development. Many of the local industrial oil magnates, such as Zeynalabdin Taghiyev, Musa Nagiyev, and Murtuza Mukhtarov, became benefactors of education and the arts, and built beautiful residences designed by European architects, many of which were later donated to charity. Today, Baku owes its European looks to these magnificent buildings of the late nineteenth and early twentieth centuries. In the early 1870s, the first Azerbaijani National Theater and the first newspaper were founded. In 1908, Baku premiered the first opera in the Muslim Orient, *Leyli and Mejnun* by U. Hajibayov.

BOOM TOWN

"As a business center, Baku has acquired considerable wealth, and the new city, which has naturally extended in all directions, contains substantially built, indeed elegant, stone houses and large shops, which would do credit to any city of Europe. The streets are rapidly being paved, and they will soon be better, in this respect, than any other town in Russia, with the exception of St. Petersburg. Evidences of wealth are not only to be seen in the appearance of the city itself, but also among many of its inhabitants."
New York Times, October 28, 1900

Thousands of people of different backgrounds from Russia and Europe were making their way to the small rural Muslim town in search of jobs and new prospects. Many of them settled, making Baku an increasingly cosmopolitan city. By 1883, the population had grown to 45,000, further expanding to 200,000 in 1913, only less than a third of whom were now ethnic Azerbaijanis.

Development of the Azerbaijani Language

The Azeri language at the time was written in Arabic script, which was not able to produce all of the Azerbaijani vowel sounds. A new trend was started by the writer Mirza Fatali Akhudov: first, to modify the Arabic script, and then to switch to the Latin alphabet, which was accomplished in 1928. The literacy rate grew steadily throughout the twentieth century, reaching nearly 100 percent by its end.

The Azerbaijani alphabet was to be changed twice more in the course of the twentieth century. In 1938, it was forcibly switched to Cyrillic (the script of the Russian language), and then, after the collapse of the Soviet Union, it reverted to Latin script in 1992. The three alphabets represent the three main components of contemporary Azeri identity—Iranian, Turkish, and Russian—but think of the effect that the changes of script had on education and of all the disruption it brought into the lives of people who found themselves illiterate overnight, when everything around them was written with letters they could not read!

The Bolsheviks

Throughout the early twentieth century, while Russia was being torn apart by the First World War and the Revolution, lawlessness was wreaking havoc in the Caucasus. Several clashes between Azeris and Armenians between 1905 and 1907 left thousands of people dead on both sides. Baku was ravaged by anarchy and was heavily involved in Bolshevik politics, which gave the city its "socialist international" image. After escaping from a Siberian prison in 1907, Stalin made Baku the base of his revolutionary activity.

Following the Bolshevik seizure of power in the October Revolution of 1917, several forces claimed power in the oil city. While the Bolsheviks declared that they were the one and only legitimate government in Baku (subordinate to Russia), the Azeri national-democrats, primarily the Musavat (Equality) party, wanted Azerbaijan to go its own way. Ethnic tensions were exacerbated by the alliance of the Bolsheviks with the Armenian Dashnak party (the Armenian Revolutionary Front).

In a bloody atrocity that started on March 31, 1918, the Armenian forces, holding the Turkic Azeris responsible for massacres perpetrated by the Ottomans against their Armenian population, went on the rampage for the next three days, killing an estimated 12,000 Muslims in Baku, most of them civilians. Today, March 31 is marked as National Genocide Day in Azerbaijan.

Azerbaijan, Armenia, and Georgia were very briefly united in an independent Transcaucasian Democratic Federative Republic in 1918, before their disagreements forced the dissolution of the union and led to their declarations of independence.

Azerbaijan Democratic Republic
On May 28, 1918, the Azerbaijan Democratic Republic was established, with its capital in Ganja, where many Azeris sought sanctuary from the violence in Baku. It was the first modern parliamentary republic in the Muslim world, and the first to extend voting rights to women. The president of the Republic, Mammad Emin Rasulzadeh, who was leader of the Musavat party, is now widely  viewed as the founding father of the modern Azerbaijani nation.

The Azerbaijan Democratic Republic was de facto recognized at the Paris Peace Conference. In August 1919, a law on Azerbaijani citizenship was enacted. Britain signed a pact with Iran, forcing it to renounce all territorial claims to Azerbaijan. However, Baku's oil proved too tempting for the new Soviet enterprise, and in 1920 the 11th Soviet Red Army invaded Azerbaijan.

The history of the short-lived Azerbaijan Democratic Republic is highly idealized by, and an inspiration to, many in modern Azerbaijan. It was also romanticized in the best-selling international

novel *Ali and Nino*, in which a prototypical noble
Azerbaijani fighter dies in battle with the invading
Bolshevik forces on the banks of the Kura River
near Ganja in 1920, and with him perishes the
hope of independent democratic Azerbaijan for
the coming decades.

Azerbaijan Soviet Socialist Republic

In 1921, Soviet Russia, Armenia, Azerbaijan, and
Georgia signed the Treaty of Kars with Turkey,
which formalized the present-day borders between
Turkey and the southern Caucasian states.

In 1922, under pressure from Moscow,
Azerbaijan, Georgia, and Armenia
were united into the Caucasus
Socialist Federative Soviet
Republic(CSFSR), part of the
newly formed USSR. Soon
after, Moscow established a
new entity in Azerbaijan's
Garabagh province, separating
the Armenian-populated
mountainous areas into the
Nagorny Karabakh Autonomous Region.

The CSFSR existed until 1936, when each of the
republics was given the status of a separate entity
within the Soviet Union. Azerbaijan became the
Azerbaijan Soviet Socialist Republic. At that time,
its alphabet was changed to Cyrillic. During the
years of Stalin's Great Purge in the 1930s,
thousands of Azerbaijanis were exiled and
executed. Much of the intellectual elite of that
time perished in the Soviet Gulags.

Azerbaijan's importance to the Soviets was mainly in its hydrocarbon resources. Baku supplied oil to help prosecute the Second World War and in 1940 production reached 72 percent of all oil extracted in the territory of the USSR. In his book *The Prize*, about the history of the oil industry, researcher Daniel Yergin writes about Hitler's plans to capture the Caucasus, specifically the oil fields of Baku, in 1942. According to some sources, a cake in the shape of the Caspian was presented to Hitler by his generals, of which he wanted the "Baku" piece.

Dissolution of the USSR

As the Soviet Union was heading into the abyss in the late 1980s, its fifteen former republics found themselves in an acute economic and political crisis. Ethnic wars were waged throughout their territories, including Azerbaijan, where the government of the autonomous region of Nagorno Karabakh, an area populated by 150,000 people, 70 percent of whom were ethnic Armenians, declared its independence from Azerbaijan and a desire for unification with neighboring Armenia. Tensions between the two Soviet Republics escalated, giving way to a mass exodus of people across the borders and to killings of Azerbaijanis and Armenians that lasted through 1994. The human cost of the war was more than 30,000 lives.

Black January

From January 13 to 16, 1990, anti-Armenian riots—fomented, it is universally believed, by the Soviet KGB—took place in Baku. During that tragic time, many Azerbaijani families hid and protected their Armenian neighbors and friends from the ravaging mobs. This gave a pretext to the Soviet government led by Mikhail Gorbachev (who, ironically, was to receive the Nobel Peace Prize during that same year) to send heavily armed troops to the city on January 20. The real reason behind the Soviet invasion was the attempt to counter the growing opposition party, the Popular Front of Azerbaijan, which was threatening to take power from the communists.

Following the scenario tested in Tbilisi in 1989 (and later repeated in Vilnius in 1991), Soviet tanks drove into the city, where hundreds of protesters had gathered in a square. In what today is known as the Black January events, the tanks were running over cars and people, and soldiers from the Special Forces opened fire indiscriminately at civilians on the streets and in their homes. More than 180 people were killed and hundreds were injured or missing. Following the carnage, a mass action of burning communist membership IDs took place on the main square of Baku. January 20 has been a day of mourning since.

First Independent Government
On October 18, 1991, the Supreme Council of Azerbaijan adopted a Declaration of Independence, confirmed by a

referendum in December 1991. The early years of independence were dominated by the Nagorno Karabakh war with Armenia (see below).

Nationalism in the region, traditionally suppressed, has been on the rise since the late 1980s. In 1988 and 1989, large crowds gathered in the biggest square in Baku, moved by Armenian territorial claims, and thus modern Azerbaijani nationalism was born, sweeping the Popular Front and its leader Abulfaz Elchibey to power in the 1992 presidential elections.

The Elchibey era is remembered by most as a moment of national euphoria and a brief period of freedom of expression and the press, but it was also a time when Baku's ethnic minorities felt compelled to leave the newly ethnocentric state, a process that reflected similar minority exoduses from the other former Soviet states.

The Nagorno Karabakh War (1991–94)

The modern states of Azerbaijan and Armenia, along with the rest of the Caucasus and Central Asia, were founded on the ruins of the Persian and Ottoman Empires, overtaken by the Russian czarist army, and later controlled by the Russian Soviet government. As soon as the central government in Moscow lost control of the situation in the two former Soviet republics, the two sides found themselves at war, rooted in mutual prejudices trailing from the previous century. The Armenians, refusing to distinguish between their archenemies, the Turks, and the Azeris, referred to ancient maps of "Greater Armenia" to claim that the Nagorno-

Karabakh region inside Azerbaijan was historically Armenian land. The Azerbaijanis had just as much historical evidence to prove that the land was rightfully theirs, and to suspect that the neighboring state was simply trying to expand its territory at the expense of Azerbaijan.

The war killed 20,000 Azerbaijanis. After taking over both the Karabakh and the surrounding Azerbaijani villages, Armenian forces ended up controlling almost 20 percent of the internationally recognized Azerbaijani territory. Azerbaijani villages surrounding Nagorno Karabakh were ethnically cleansed of 600,000 Azeri inhabitants, who joined the 200,000 ethnic Azeris who had fled Armenia proper between 1987 and 1988. Their total number made Azerbaijan the country with the highest per capita number of refugees in the world (10 percent of the population).

Four UN resolutions in 1993, calling for the unconditional withdrawal of Armenian troops from the occupied lands, have been ignored and Armenian forces continue to control Nagorno Karabakh, along with the areas around it. The only way to get to Karabakh today is through the newly created Lachin land corridor from Armenia. The official policy of the Azerbaijani government is to deny visas to tourists who have visited Nagorno Karabakh via Armenia because this represents an unauthorized entry into Azerbaijan's territory, and also because the safety of those tourists who do this cannot be guaranteed.

Since signing a cease-fire in 1994, Azerbaijan has been unable to recapture any of its occupied lands and the government, having expanded its military budget by more than 1,000 percent in the past decade, continuously threatens to retake them by force if Armenia does not agree to return them peacefully.

Information Warfare

While losing the war with Armenia in the battlefield in the early 1990s, Azerbaijan also found itself on the losing side of the information war. An isolated and inexperienced post-Soviet orphan in the "globalized" system of relationships, Azerbaijan was up against the sophisticated and powerful international Armenian Diaspora, especially in the United States, who were actively lobbying in favor of post-Soviet Armenia.

In the years that have passed since, Azerbaijan has undertaken a rigorous effort to support a national Diaspora around the world, including Russia, the USA, and Europe, to offset the Armenian lead in the international political and information battles. A Committee on Diaspora Issues has been formed, with the aim of introducing international opinion makers to Azerbaijan.

The New "Oil Boom"

After a series of military coups, power was taken in 1993 by Azerbaijan's former communist leader and member of the Soviet Politburo, Heydar Aliyev. In two major milestones in the country's recent history,

he signed a cease-fire with the advancing Armenians
in 1994, and in the same year sealed what is known
as the Contract of the Century with a consortium of
Western oil companies led by British Petroleum for
the development of the Azerbaijani oil fields. In the
fifteen years since, nearly 200 million tons of oil have
been extracted, increasing Azerbaijan's budget nearly
forty times over. His son Ilham Aliyev is the current
president of Azerbaijan.

THE ECONOMY
The cornerstone of the economy is the
hydrocarbon industry. Partly due to the rise of oil
prices, in 2007 Azerbaijan had the world's fastest
growing economy, with GDP expanding at 41.7
percent. In 2009, GDP grew 9.3 percent; however,
non-oil related sectors saw a more modest growth
of 3 percent (down from 16 percent in 2008).
Azerbaijan has repaid most of its IMF debt and
announced plans to become completely debt free
by 2014.

THE ENVIRONMENT

The development of oil by the Soviets led to the creation of several environmental disaster zones around Baku. Other sources of pollution in Azerbaijan are industrial plants and the dumping of waste into the Caspian Sea.

The famous Caspian sturgeon is becoming extinct due to overfishing and poaching in all neighboring states, which have started taking measures to prevent the decline in the fish's numbers. Stricter controls of the waters, measures against poachers, and new fish farms are some of the small steps taken by their respective governments, working against time while the sturgeon population is quickly diminishing. The combination of scarcity and tighter fishing regulations has caused caviar prices in Baku to rise accordingly in less than a decade, from a meager US$10 for a 1 pound (nearly 500 g) jar in the 1990s, which made caviar a popular souvenir for travelers, to more than US$150 for a small 4 oz (113 g) container nowadays.

chapter two

VALUES & ATTITUDES

"We were a very mixed lot, we forty schoolboys who were having a geography lesson one hot afternoon in the Imperial Russian Humanistic High School of Baku, Transcaucasia: thirty Mohammedans, four Armenians, two Poles, three Sectarians, and one Russian. So far we had not given much thought to the extraordinary geographical position of our town but now Professor Sanin was telling us in his flat and uninspired way: 'The eastern border of Europe goes through the Russian Empire, along the Ural Mountains, through the Caspian Sea and through Transcaucasia. Some scholars look at the area south of the Caucasian mountains as belonging to Asia, while others, in view of Transcaucasia's cultural evolution, believe that this country should be considered part of Europe. It can therefore be said, my children, that it is partly your responsibility as to whether our town should belong to progressive Europe or to reactionary Asia.'"

Kurban Said, *Ali and Nino*, 1937

THE AZERI *MENTALITET*

With its eclectic nature acknowledged by Western researchers, Azerbaijani national identity, influenced by centuries of external conquests and internal struggles, today finds itself at many cultural crossroads. The key to understanding modern Azerbaijani values lies in accepting the diversity of influences that have contributed to the makeup of the nation.

In an article in the *Azerbaijan International* magazine, a former French Ambassador to the country, the Orientalist Jean Pierre Guinhut, writes that Azerbaijan ". . . has always been at the crossroads of Oriental influence. It is an ancient cultural settlement with a long-standing inclination for lyric arts. On the other hand, it has absorbed much of the heritage of Europe, which embraces a tolerant and modernistic attitude towards both religion and culture."

Civil discourse in Azerbaijan today frequently turns to the question of what constitutes the national character, with compatriots discussing its quirks online, publishing impassioned articles in the media, and writing books and scholarly monographs on the subject. *Mentalitet* (or mentality) is one of the most popular words used by professionals and laymen alike as a justification for nearly everything—be it conformity to tradition, importance of family, political inertia, modesty, artistry, or tolerance of corruption. Whether the subject of discussion is a matter of pride or shame, *mentalitet* always serves as a feasible explanation.

In his book *The Archetypal Azeris: Faces of Mentality*, published in 2000, the Azerbaijani scholar Hasan Kuliyev discussed important aspects of the Azerbaijani ethnic tradition and its adaptation to a modern urban setting, exacerbated by decades of suppression and brutal political changes that have affected the existing social order. The post-Soviet age of uncertainty, in particular, has left a mark on rapidly transforming attitudes.

Despite significant changes in the political, economic, and social order, some values are shared by most Azerbaijanis. Family values are among the most cherished, including devotion to children and respect for the older generation, in particular reverence for mothers. Other important values are hospitality, women's honor and modesty, and a tradition of strong leadership and authority, along with a certain degree of unruliness and rebellion.

FAMILY TIES

The Azerbaijanis' main devotion and loyalty is to their families. Family networks are strong and flexible and family members expect and offer mutual assistance, time, and resources throughout their lives. Extended families are close and cousins are often referred to as brothers and sisters.

"Relatives may eat your flesh but they won't throw away your bones" is an old saying meant to remind us that, exasperating as family relations may be at times, they are the most stable of all social ties in Azerbaijan and one can count on them until the last days of one's life.

Life without children would seem meaningless to most Azerbaijanis, regardless of their professional achievements and social status. Once married, the newlyweds are expected to become parents soon and to continue the life cycle. It is important to have a male descendant to continue the family line and to preserve the family's last name, and many couples make numerous attempts to conceive a boy.

Parents are expected to provide support for their children well past their twenty-first birthdays, and children, in turn, rarely disobey their parents when making important life decisions. Usually, moms and dads provide their married offspring with housing, either by helping to buy new apartments or by sharing their own living quarters.

The post-Soviet changes in the economy, however, left many impoverished and there has been a reverse trend in which the modern young, who have well-paid jobs, support their parents financially.

THE ROLE OF WOMEN

Women occupy an important place in the Azerbaijani psyche. Their main job is to serve their families by being exemplary wives and mothers, even if they have full-time jobs outside the home. In addition, women have the symbolic role of keepers of the family honor.

The standards of female behavior are described by Farideh Heyat, author of the research-based book *Azeri Women in Transition*. A glance at the glossary reveals the existence of such terms in the

Azeri language as *haya* (female shame), *gheirat* (dignity, male honor), and *namus* (male honor related to female sexual propriety), all pointing to the importance of women in protecting the men's honor. A loss of honor by a woman automatically brings anathema upon her male relatives, who are supposed to take action to prevent the dishonoring behavior in the future and/or to disown the disgraced female. In the most severe cases, honor killings can happen. Men's behavior, on the other hand, is guided by the unwritten code of *kishilik*, or manhood, which, among other things, requires them to keep family females under strict control.

Dress Codes

Throughout the twentieth century, there has been a gradual process of liberalization of the female dress

code. It went from the traditional head-to-toe cover of the *chadra* in the early 1900s to revealing tops with miniskirts and flashy makeup just one hundred years

later. Early Soviet-era cartoons often ridiculed the *chadra* as a representation of backward traditions.

A monument to a woman discarding her veil stands prominently in a central location of Baku, but the *hijab* (head scarf) is becoming fashionable.

The collapse of Soviet communism has facilitated the reentry of religion into social life and some women choose to cover their heads again, while some (albeit only a few so far) cover their entire bodies. The newly veiled women range from ardent adherents of the Islamic tradition to those who view it as an attractive addition to their identity. Their

Soviet-raised parents and grandparents are often perplexed by young women's choice to wear a veil.

Women's Rights
Paradoxically, the years after the Soviet demise have seen both a significant rise in the number of women who have taken on the role of breadwinners and a rapid deterioration in the position of women and girls in spheres where they had traditionally been more advanced. In the Soviet Union, access to education, along with protective labor legislation and government-supported child care, opened new economic and political doors to women. An equivalent of the American "affirmative action" program assigned a quota for the number of women and ethnic minorities in parliament, proportional to the general population. The Soviet Azerbaijan's Supreme Soviet (the parliament) was 39 percent women. This figure dropped to 11 percent in post-Soviet Azerbaijan.

The ability of women to work while the state cares for their children has diminished greatly. Women often stay at home to take care of young children, but many have to earn a living and return to work, even though the law provides a generous maternity leave of three years.

Schools in the south of Azerbaijan, near the border with Iran, now have few girls enrolled beyond the age of puberty, and the number of underage marriages in the region has grown. On the other hand, many women in villages in the north of the country have had to take on a leading role as their husbands have moved to Russia in search of better economic opportunities.

HOSPITALITY AND GENEROSITY

Hospitality is one of the cornerstone values of every Azerbaijani family. Azerbaijanis are skilled hosts and it is customary even for people of humble means to offer the utmost of what they have to their guests. Traditionally, a guest should be given the best room in the house, served the best food, and showered with attention.

Extreme Hospitality

There is a popular Azerbaijani myth about the sanctity of guests, according to which, if a guest happens to insult the host by killing his brother, the host must nevertheless show the utmost courtesy while the guest is still in his house. It is only after the guest steps outside that the host can get even.

These requirements of hospitality stem from the broader Azerbaijani respect for generosity as one of life's main virtues. Bighearted gestures, such as paying for an entire table of friends dining at a restaurant or other costly favors for friends and guests, are still a norm, even after two decades of economic hardship that have limited most people's financial capabilities. Thrift and financial prudence are not accorded the same respect as in the West, and most people value the short-term pleasure of entertaining their friends more highly than longer-term financial planning.

The generosity shown toward friends is expected to be paid back some day, however. A recent survey showed that most Azerbaijani respondents valued relatives and friends of high social status as a more important source of their own personal welfare than money or good jobs. Sociologists have suggested that this is the result of the perceived transience of jobs and money as opposed to the more permanent and reliable links with friends and relatives.

REGIONALISM

Azerbaijani social relations and current politics depend heavily on regional identity. Regional dialects are easily spotted by a trained ear and folktales assign various qualities to people hailing from different regions. "*Haralisan*?" ("Where are you from?") is one of the most frequent questions that people either ask directly or imply indirectly when they meet a new compatriot.

Regionalism has been particularly strong in clan-based post-Soviet Azerbaijani politics, with some groups gaining the upper hand and filling important government jobs and most administrative positions.

GISMET / FATE

Azerbaijanis rarely talk about the future (be it the next day or next year) without adding "*Insh-Allah*," or "God willing!" Most Azerbaijanis are highly fatalistic and firmly believe that personal will is only applicable when destiny is benevolent. Inexorable fate is not subject to change—everyone has their *gismet* predetermined by the higher powers.

WORK ETHIC

Azerbaijanis are hardworking and assertive in defending their right to make a living for their families. A popular saying, "*Bajarana jan gurban*," which means "Blessed be the one who can," reflects the importance of a "can do" attitude, especially if it brings clear dividends, often irrespective of the means employed to achieve the desired ends.

Ethnic Azerbaijani communities in the rural areas of Russia are usually more pragmatic and often better off financially than their Russian neighbors.

ATTITUDES TO TIME

While time may be viewed as a commodity in some cultures, Azerbaijanis rarely stick to the clock and to agreed-on deadlines. Dates set for the implementation of projects are largely symbolic rather than set in stone. "We will get there when we get there" is a common attitude.

Deadlines are certainly not as important as developing relationships. If an Azerbaijani en route to a meeting encounters a friend, he is likely to spend some time asking how they are and responding to similar questions, even if it makes him late for his meeting. It would be unthinkable to rush by, uttering excuses about lack of time, without at least a short verbal exchange.

COMMUNAL OR INDIVIDUALIST?

In most spheres of life Azerbaijanis conform strictly to communal values. Yet some aspects of their behavior can be extremely individualistic. On one hand, people are very oriented toward the group—actions are rarely taken without regard to how they will be perceived by society. On the other, there is often little respect for public space and public property, and people driving or waiting in line can be blatantly disregarded by their fellow countrymen trying to muscle in.

The key to understanding the roots of these contradictions lies in deciphering who is considered to be valuable and part of an "in-group." Researchers suggest that the level of interpersonal trust in Azerbaijani society is low, as is trust in most institutions. So people place their trust in the immediate and extended family. Other people who count are friends, colleagues, and close neighbors with whom one interacts daily.

In rural areas, the entire village community is considered important. During elections in remote villages it is not uncommon to see communities voting in clusters—a respected leader of the village decides the voting choice and passes it down to the rest of community.

RESPECT AND STATUS

Status, determined by a person's age and, increasingly, wealth and links to important people, is a significant factor in regulating social relationships, and the demonstration of respect is an important virtue in the minds of Azerbaijanis.

It is customary for the oldest (or otherwise most respected) person in the family or any other group to act as a mediator in disputes and to be asked for advice on important matters. The word *agsakkal*, which means "white-bearded," is widely used to describe a wise elder. If someone in the family seeks to make a decision about an important matter, such as marriage or the purchase of a house, without consulting—and thus showing respect to—a member of the older generation, it is likely to be perceived as an insult.

The young are expected to greet elders first and will usually rise when such a person enters the room. It is customary to offer one's seat to an older passenger on public transportation.

SHOWING EMOTIONS

Azerbaijanis are often joyful and jolly, making puns and jokes with their friends and family. However, the rules of social engagement dictate emotional restraint around strangers. The accepted standard of behavior for a man who wants to be taken seriously is to maintain a dignified bearing, called *samballi* in Azeri. To be unnecessarily cheerful in public means to lose face. Public activists and government figures add weight to their personas by looking stern and unsmiling on promotional photos. (However, the savviest of them understand that they need to smile when posing for the media on their visits to Western shores.)

In very traditional families, it is unacceptable for husbands and wives to hold hands, embrace, or otherwise demonstrate affection in the presence of their parents or other elderly people. Men should also maintain their masculine dignity by refraining from kissing children. Similarly, for women, an extreme show of joy can be interpreted as an unwelcome lack of modesty. A display of sorrow, however, is widely accepted. Mourning widows are supposed to cry and otherwise display extreme sadness. Emotional restraint among women at the death of loved ones is considered inappropriate.

SHAME AND HONOR

Every Azerbaijani has a deeply ingrained sense of the community's role in pointing out what's right and wrong, and individualism is actively discouraged through shaming. Shame plays an important role in the social order. The modern Azerbaijani language has many phrases that reflect the fear of being judged unfavorably by others, such as "I'll be laughed at" or "What will people say?"

The importance of establishing a reputation is hard to overestimate. Acting in a way deemed inappropriate by the community brings disgrace not just on the individual in question but on his or her entire family—a serious matter, as family lineage is a crucial part of Azerbaijani social life. There are some examples of self-made men and women who have risen to prominence, but having the right family background considerably smoothes the process.

LINEAGE
A typical introduction of someone from a prominent clan may include flowery pronouncements of their ancestral achievements. In Baku, it is particularly prestigious to hail from a family of the urban intelligentsia and to have a surname that includes the suffixes bey or khan, used by nobility in the pre-Soviet days.

INDIRECTNESS AND SAVING FACE
Indirectness is an important part of local etiquette. Rather than issuing criticism to someone's face, a mediator is usually asked to deliver the news. A popular saying, "I say this to my daughter, so that my daughter-in-law will hear," means that many

things said in one's presence often have an underlying meaning. Deciphering these hidden messages can be an exhausting task even for a person skilled at reading the tea leaves of indirect communication, but for a newcomer they may sometimes become overwhelming.

Blushes Spared

The way of asking for a woman's hand still involves the family of the would-be groom visiting her parents, where they are served traditional tea. Whether the tea is sweetened or not signals to the visitors if the woman's family is willing to join their kin by allowing the marriage to take place. If, for whatever reason, the answer is a "no," the tea is not sweetened and both families are spared the humiliation of a direct rejection.

chapter three

FESTIVALS & TRADITIONS

CELEBRATING AT HOME

Traditionally, Azerbaijanis spend their holidays at home with family and guests. Women cook elaborate dishes for feasts that start in the evening and often last well into the night. Extended family members pay visits and give presents to each other. Many people in Baku who have family in the regions travel to visit them and to make the rounds in the villages.

While entertaining guests at home is still a sign of the utmost respect, it is also becoming increasingly fashionable among the urban upper and middle classes to gather in restaurants, thus avoiding all the hard work that goes into cooking and hosting a party. Restaurant and café reservations for New Year's Eve in Baku, for instance, fill up well in advance.

FLEXIBLE SCHEDULES

Days off for national holidays are usually shifted around to line up more days in a row. For example, if a holiday falls on a Tuesday, the government may make a last-minute announcement that the day off is being moved to the Monday. Holidays that coincide with weekends are compensated for with extra days off just before or after the weekend

The announcements of the exact dates always come at very short notice, which can make early holiday planning quite challenging, added to by the uncertainty surrounding the precise dates of religious Muslim holidays, which change every year according to the lunar calendar (the central mosque makes an announcement a day or two before the day itself, based on sighting of the moon)

HOLIDAYS OLD AND NEW

Throughout Azerbaijan's recent history competing historical narratives have been reinforced in the public's mind through discarded, resurrected, and newly invented commemorations. Hence, holidays may sometimes get caught up in political controversy.

Azerbaijan's calendar today has seventeen official holidays, including three days of mourning. A few holidays are eagerly anticipated and widely celebrated in homes and on the streets. Others, in the several years since their inception, are still making their way into people's hearts and minds.

BIRTHDAYS

The least controversial of celebrations are birthdays. (Even though the few ardent followers of Islamic tradition argue that a person's birth date has little importance in the eyes of God.) Special dates, such as fiftieth or sixtieth jubilees, are celebrated most lavishly, often in one of the ubiquitous *shadliq sarayi* or *shadliq evi* (palaces or houses of joy, respectively).

Whether held at home or in a restaurant, birthday parties always involve flowers, presents, and dressing up. If you are invited to a birthday party, make sure to bring a bouquet, especially for a birthday girl. Traditionally, presents are not opened immediately in the presence of the giver. If you see your present casually tossed into a pile of other gifts, remember that this is meant to emphasize its relative unimportance compared to the joy of seeing you.

Young children's "important" birthdays (such as a baby turning one) are often used as an occasion for parents and grandparents to have a party for relatives, colleagues, and acquaintances. If you have been invited to a "baby party" and are planning to bring along your own kids, make sure to ask the hosts if other children have been invited as well, as they may not have anything planned for their entertainment. Gold and money are the most popular presents for the occasion. However, for slightly older children, the new trend is to organize restaurant parties with clowns and loud disco music.

NATIONAL HOLIDAYS
January 1–2, New Year
The New Year celebrations in Baku are elaborate, with a giant New Year tree on the main square, massive fireworks, and a late-night party on the square featuring performances by many of the country's celebrities, starting at around 9:00 p.m. on December 31 and lasting through the small hours of the morning on January 1. The amplified sound of a ticking clock counts out the last seconds of the outgoing year and most families celebrating at home and watching the show on TV have their glasses of champagne at the ready at midnight. It is customary to congratulate everyone by saying, "*Yeni Iliniz Mubarak*" and by wishing them a good year ahead.

March 8, Women's Day
International Women's Day was first celebrated in Azerbaijan in 1917 (and has been a day off since 1965) but over time it transformed from a political holiday dedicated to promoting equal rights for women into a sexist manifestation of special treatment for the "representatives of the weaker sex," a definition that its founder, the German revolutionary Clara Zetkin, would likely find objectionable.

In its contemporary form, Women's Day resembles a combination of Valentine's Day and Mother's Day. The obligatory bunches of flowers for mothers, wives, daughters, female cousins, teachers, and colleagues drive flower prices sky high on March 8 and on the few preceding days.

On Women's Day, it is customary for men to demonstrate chivalry, compliment women on their looks, wish them eternal beauty, and offer chocolates, presents, and flowers to significant females in their lives.

March 20–24, Novruz Bayrami

The most significant Azerbaijani holiday is the traditional celebration of the arrival of spring,

which signifies the beginning of a new year. This 3,000-year-old Zoroastrian holiday coincides with the vernal equinox on March 21. Novruz (also known as Nowrouz, Nooruz, Navruz, Nauroz, or Nevruz in other countries that celebrate it) was added to UNESCO's Representative List of the Intangible Cultural Heritage of Humanity in 2009.

Street festivities in Baku's main tourist destinations continue for several days and include centuries-old traditional crowd-pleasers such as weightlifters (*pehlevans*) and wire walkers, along with musicians, theatrical performances, and stalls

with arts and crafts for sale. Actors dressed as characters from well-known Azerbaijani plays and films walk around the Old City streets and pose for pictures.

The four Tuesdays preceding March 21 are celebrated with bonfires, over which kids and adults jump to have their wishes come true. The last of the Tuesdays, Akhir Chershenbe, is a day of festivities and feasts.

Homes are decorated with *semeni*, bowls of wheat sprouts that are prepared weeks in advance of the holiday, with trays full of dried fruits and nuts, and often painted eggs and candles. Neighbors exchange plates of traditional

pastries—*pakhlava, shekerbura, gogal.* Usually, the females of the extended family get together for several days to make these labor-intensive treats with nuts, butter, and honey, but for working women, unable to invest hours of work in the process, there is the option of buying them ready-made.

If someone (likely, a neighbor) gives you a plate with traditional offerings, it is customary to return it not empty but bearing something symbolic, such as a few pieces of candy or fruit.

May 9, Victory Day
This day commemorates the moment when the victorious Soviet troops raised the Soviet flag over the Reichstag in 1945, thereby bringing an end to the Great Patriotic War against Nazi Germany, known elsewhere as the Second World War. Among the tens of millions of Soviet citizens who perished during the war were many Azerbaijanis. Baku ensured crucial oil supplies for the war effort.

One of the most important holidays in the USSR, it was cancelled briefly as "too Russian" by the nationalist government of Abulfaz Elchibey, but later May 9 was reinstated as one of Azerbaijan's national holidays. Nevertheless, there isn't much fanfare around it nowadays, with only a few Second World War veterans still alive and many of them impoverished. In 2010, a presidential decree added 30 manats (about US$40) to their monthly allowance. The

Azerbaijan Veterans Council and the Russian Embassy in Baku also present war veterans with small amounts of cash.

May 10, Flower Festival

The Flower Festival was established by the mayor's office of Baku in 2004, as the birthday celebration of President Heydar Aliyev, who died in December 2003. Although not an official day off, the holiday is lavishly celebrated. The city's main parks are lined with elaborate flower and tree installations and the evening features a gala concert at the seaside.

May 28, Republic Day

On this day in 1918, the fledgling independent government declared the short-lived Azerbaijan Democratic Republic. This holiday replaces the now discarded April 28, celebrated for most of the Soviet years, the date of the Bolshevik troops' arrival in Baku in 1920.

June 15, National Salvation Day

Marks the day when Heydar Aliyev, also known as the National Leader of Azerbaijan, came to Baku in 1993 to lead Azerbaijan into its petro-prosperous future.

June 26, National Army and Navy Day

Commemorates the date in 1918 when the national army was founded by the Azerbaijan Democratic Republic's government.

October 18, National Independence Day
On this day in 1991, Azerbaijan declared its independence from the Soviet Union.

November 9, National Flag Day
This is a new holiday, celebrated for the first time in 2010. In September 2010, Azerbaijan installed the world's highest flagpole, as recorded in the *Guinness Book of Records.*

November 12, Constitution Day
The first post-Soviet constitution was adopted after a nationwide referendum in 1995.

November 17, National Revival Day
The day marks the start of the national movement in 1988 when thousands of protesters gathered in Baku's main square to call for an end to the Soviet bias against Azerbaijan, after the Soviet government failed to react to the expulsion of 200,000 ethnic Azeris from their homes in Armenia and to the killing of Azeris in the Nagorno Karabakh region of Azerbaijan.

December 31, Day of Solidarity of World Azerbaijanis
A celebration of ethnic brotherhood, the Day of Azerbaijani Solidarity is a nice excuse for most people to add a off day to the New Year's holiday. On that day in 1989, part of the Soviet-Iranian border was demolished by Azerbaijani nationalists, who declared unity with their brethren across the border.

MUSLIM HOLIDAYS (Dates change according to the lunar calendar)

The two main Islamic holidays celebrated in Azerbaijan are Kurban Bayrami and Ramazan Bayrami.

Kurban Bayrami (Eid el-Adha)

This day commemorates the sacrifice of a ram by Abraham in place of his son. Thousands of sheep are raised especially for the occasion and ritually slaughtered near places of worship as well as in backyards and on streets. The meat is distributed to the poor or to family members.

Ramazan Bayrami (Eid ul-Fitr)

This is the feast celebrating the end of the month of fasting, Ramadan. The number of Azerbaijanis who fast during Ramadan grows with every year, and survey data suggest that almost 50 percent of respondents fast at least for some time. The faithful demonstrate self-restraint and patience from dawn to sunset by abstaining from food, drink, and cigarettes. The daily fast ends with a prayer followed by a joyful meal called *iftar*.

The month of Ramadan is also a time of quiet self-reflection, during which people pray, abstain from having sex, and try to avoid arguing or thinking troublesome thoughts.

DAYS OF MOURNING

On days of national mourning, TV and radio networks replace their regular programming with appropriately grave pieces of classical music, and local restaurants do not offer live music and other entertainment.

January 20, Black January

The day marks the invasion of Baku by Soviet tanks in 1990. Usually, the president, flanked by top government officials and followed by tens of thousands of civilians, visits and lays a wreath at the Alley of the Fallen, located on top of a hill overlooking Baku Bay, where the Black January victims are buried. The procession and ceremony are aired live on all local TV channels.

February 26, Day of the Khojali Genocide

A major Armenian offensive during the war in Nagorno Karabakh took place in the village of

Khojali in 1992; more than six hundred civilians were slaughtered by the Armenian forces, backed up by a Russian tank unit.

Graphic images of the decapitated bodies of children, women, and the elderly penetrate the Azerbaijani print and broadcast media. These images, which fuel passions around the shared national grief, were taken by a group of Azeri journalists headed by a cameraman named Chingiz Mustafayev, who was later killed in the war zone. The radio station ANS-ChM, part of the Azerbaijani News Service, a major media group, is named after him.

The Need for Sensitivity
In 2006, in an unprecedented strike, more than a thousand local Azerbaijani workers on a BP rig construction facility refused to return to work after two British managers outraged them by removing a newsletter with the disturbing Khojali images from a commemoration wall in one of the contractors' offices. After a public apology the managers were removed from their positions, and left the country soon after.

March 31, Day of the Genocide of Azerbaijanis
March 31 was established as national Genocide Day by presidential decree in 2002. The date refers to the Baku events of March

1918 when thousands of Azeri Muslims were massacred by joint Armenian and Bolshevik forces.

Meherremlik and Ashura

The Islamic New Year (the first day of Muharram, the first month of the Islamic lunar calendar) is anything but a happy occasion in Shi'a Azerbaijan. Meherremlik is a month of mourning and fasting, which culminates on the tenth day of the following month (Ashura) by commemorating the martyrdom of the Prophet's grandson, Imam Husseyn. The self-flagellating ritual of Shahsey-Vahsey, when Shi'a fanatics strive

to ceremonially whip their bare chests and backs, is actively discouraged by the government, and mosques throughout the country ask believers to donate blood instead. Weddings and other large celebrations are usually not scheduled for the month of Meherremlik.

WEDDINGS AND FUNERALS

These life cycle events are occasions for extended family members to see and greet each other. Azeris often say, "*Toylarda ve yaslarda gorushuruk*" ("We only meet at weddings and funerals").

Weddings

In the family-focused life of Azerbaijanis, weddings have a special place. One of the most important communal rituals in the life of every family, a wedding (*toy*) is a major event that requires a significant investment of time and resources. It is not uncommon even for families of modest means to borrow heavily in order to arrange big weddings for their children. The number of large restaurants where people celebrate weddings (*shadliq sarayi*) has grown exponentially in the last two decades.

A traditional Azeri wedding consists of two parts: the official procedure of becoming a husband and wife at a government registry, and the following lavish party at the *shadliq sarayi* for hundreds of relatives and friends of the newlyweds. Long rows of tables are laid with a variety of cold starters, and waiters continuously make the rounds with trays from which they serve main course dishes. Music is usually very loud, so don't plan on talking to the person sitting next to you. Everyone is expected to enjoy themselves by eating and performing energetic national and disco dances.

Guests who want to share their greetings with everyone approach the master of ceremonies and, in the short breaks between music, he introduces the speakers and gives them a chance to make a toast.

The bride and groom, flanked by their respective witnesses, are perched at a separate table on a pedestal facing the party hall. Arriving guests head there with greetings before finding their seats at the tables. The most common phrase to wish the newlyweds a long happy life together is "*Khoshbakht Olun!*"

As weddings are such lavish occasions, to help offset their high costs, instead of presents everyone brings an envelope with cash, usually around US$100 a person (more for close friends and relatives). There will be either someone at the entrance who will collect the money and ask for your name and whether you are the bride's or the groom's guest, or, as is more widespread nowadays, there will be a box with envelopes that you can use for your donation. Remember to write your name on it before dropping it in.

Circumcision

Azeri Muslim boys undergo the ritual of circumcision (*sunnet*) usually at the age of one but it can be some years later. Called a "small wedding" (*kichik toy*), the party to celebrate a boy becoming a man is a moment of great joy and pride for the family and the party can be as large as a real wedding. It is customary to give money as a present.

Funerals (*Yas*)

According to Muslim tradition, the dead must be buried before sunset, either on the same day or, if there isn't enough time to make all the necessary preparations, on the next day.

Women are not allowed to participate in the burial ceremony because it is believed that their spirits may disturb the dead, whose souls are in a transitory state for forty days after death. After forty days, women may start visiting the graveyard. They should cover their heads.

The Azeri phrase to say to both men and women who have been bereaved is "*Allah Rehmet Elesin*," which means "May God accept his/her soul."

The home of the deceased is generally open for visits every day for forty days but the assigned days for the expression of condolences are the third, the seventh, and the fortieth days after death, and every Thursday before the fortieth day. A special funeral dish (*halva*) is cooked from flour, sugar, and butter, and served to the visitors with tea. You have to eat a small piece. Usually, a full meal is served as well. Women and men visit separately, in the mornings and afternoons respectively.

It is not customary to bring anything on these occasions, although close friends and relatives help offset the cost by giving money to the person funding the funeral expenses.

Christian and Jewish families, of course, follow their own traditions.

chapter four

MAKING FRIENDS

Making friends in Azerbaijan can be the easiest or the most daunting of tasks, depending on your particular circumstances, such as gender, age, status, and the length of your visit, and on the dynamics of the situation.

Initially, your new acquaintances may seem overly friendly and always ready to help—which to them is likely to be an expression of hospitality—but you will soon realize that you need time to win their trust before being added to the ranks of "true friends." An Azerbaijani proverb says of friends tested by time, "Everything is best new, but friendship is best old."

Many friendships formed in school and college last a lifetime. As people get older, it becomes increasingly difficult for them to cement a friendship with the people they meet. Overall, Azerbaijanis often shun strangers and are a little cautious when interacting with casual acquaintances who do not come from the trusted circle of their family connections.

Many young people have turned to the Internet to connect with others sharing similar interests and to find marriage partners, but this method of meeting new friends is still not widespread, even among younger Azerbaijanis.

The difference between friends and acquaintances, often blurred in Western cultures, is very clear to Azerbaijanis. The most important distinction is the total commitment and frequent contact of real friendship. Even though an Azeri proverb says, "A friend is still a friend, even if you haven't seen him for many years," it is unusual for Azerbaijanis to remain out of touch with their friends for a long time.

One is expected to make frequent contact with close buddies and ask often about their life and well-being. If a friend has problems, it is not enough to express concern but also customary to offer help and advice. A friend will usually call and ask about new developments until the situation is resolved.

PRIVACY AND PERSONAL SPACE

As you can imagine, all this translates into very little privacy and personal space. Close friends, just like family, are entitled to know everything about you, expect to be confided in when you make important decisions, and want you to be available for them.

An Azerbaijani couple who returned to Baku after a few years in the United States described their experience of differences in the nature of friendship across cultures in an article published in the *Azerbaijan International* magazine. While living away from Azerbaijan, they had grown used to enjoying their privacy and not having unannounced guests, but upon their return to Baku, they had to relearn the rules of visiting and hospitality, which require cheerfully accommodating big groups of friends at very short notice, should they choose to visit at any time, stay late, and perhaps spend a night.

Desire for personal space and solitude is not easily understood. Part of the feeling that locals have for visiting foreigners is pity for someone who may be suffering from being lonely. This is especially true in the countryside. The Azerbaijani word *darikhmag* conveys a set of meanings that include being bored, feeling uneasy, and being lonely. The author of a Public Radio International audio story, Carla Seidl, who lived in Azerbaijan in 2008, visited her friend's family in a village and was offered a present of farm eggs still covered with chicken poop. When she walked in, Carla was greeted with a question by her hostess, "*Darikhmirsan ki, Karla?*" This did not get translated in the sound bite on the radio, but was meant to ask whether she was feeling lonely, away from home, friends, and loved ones. The eggs, still warm from under the chicken, were to share some of the warmth of home life with her.

ATTITUDES TO FOREIGNERS

Azerbaijanis are naturally drawn to foreigners and curious about their lives. Expect to be asked a lot of questions, including details of your personal life. If you happen to be unmarried, they will probably ask the reason and sometimes even try to find a suitable match. If you are a married female without children, they will be genuinely concerned about you and offer their sympathy.

Remember that you are likely to be perceived as an ambassador of your country. Standards of behavior for foreigners and locals differ vastly. What may not be appropriate for a local person will be accepted from visitors as "their way," with the exception of blatant breaches of social norms, most often related to sexuality and dress code.

Attracting Attention

To many first-time visitors to Azerbaijan, especially obvious Western tourists, the level of attention to their humble selves may seem discomforting but the reason for stares is mostly unthreatening curiosity. What often makes Westerners visible among locals is their brightly colored clothing (most locals prefer wearing black, especially in the winter). Other giveaway items are shorts on men, running shoes on people of both sexes, and casual, low-key outfits for women.

INVITATIONS HOME

Even as a very new acquaintance, you are likely to be invited home, often at short notice. You will probably be treated to tea with sweets, often followed by a meal ranging from a few dishes to a lavish spread.

Be My Guest!

One of the most frequently used Azeri phrases is "*Gonag Ol!*" ("Be my guest!") It should not always be taken literally. For example, if you share a taxi ride with an Azeri acquaintance who is being dropped off first, he or she is likely to part from you with the required "*Gonag Ol*" without the expectation that you will accept the invitation.

The phrase "*Gonag Ol!*" is also sometimes used by service people in response to questions about payment (meaning, "It's a gift and you owe

nothing"). They don't actually mean it; they are just
being polite. You need to play along and ask again
to get a reluctant direct answer.

When visiting, take a small gift for your
hosts. You cannot go wrong with flowers
and boxes of chocolate for women and a
small toy for a child. If you know for sure
that your new friends drink alcohol, you
can bring a bottle. Men prefer vodka; wine
is usually considered a drink for women who may
only raise a glass with visiting guests. In more
conservative families, women don't drink at all.

After stepping inside, remember to start
removing your shoes at the door. If your hosts do
not want you to bother, they will tell you so;
otherwise they will offer you slippers. Shoes that
have walked the streets of Baku become dusty very
quickly and many city dwellers try to protect their
carpets by keeping slippers at the ready for visitors.
The roots of this tradition in Muslim countries go
back to the times when people slept, ate, and most
importantly, prayed on carpets.

The woman of the house will often serve guests
throughout the evening, rarely sitting down to
share the meal and conversation. She will change
your plates at least once, usually between starters
and the main course. Plastic or paper plates and
utensils are a no-no in Azeri homes.

When "No" Means "Yes"
Expect to be offered drinks and food several times
after you decline. It is considered polite to refuse an

offer two or three times before accepting it, and your hosts may assume that you, too, are just being courteous or shy. An Azerbaijani "no" often means "yes" if you ask enough times.

The dinner is likely to last the whole evening, with several courses, many offerings of a second helping, toasts, and jokes. You are likely to be honored in numerous flowery toasts, so if you feel comfortable speaking, it will be appropriate to ask your hosts for permission to say a few words and then to raise a glass to their hospitality and wish their family prosperity and peace.

You can compliment the hostess on her delicious food and express admiration for the skill and time it must have taken to prepare the spread but, if you are a man, avoid complimenting the women of the house on their appearance. Some more conservative men, who try to protect women from interaction with the outside world, may take your comments as an insult to their honor.

ENTERTAINING

Keep in mind that inviting your friends to dine outside the home may sometimes make them uncomfortable because the rules of hospitality require them to pay for guests and visitors and they may not always be able to afford it. Also, the older generation may not be accustomed to the relatively new tradition of frequently dining out; in Soviet times the absolute majority of people had their meals at home, while restaurants were viewed mainly as places of entertainment.

If you are hosting the dinner at your home and inviting your local friends, remember to keep a few spare pairs of slippers handy and to insist on offering your guests food and drink more than once. Also be prepared for them to arrive dressed up and laden with presents. Azeri families rarely invite each other to dinner without a formal reason (such as a birthday or a notable happening in the family), and the gatherings usually follow the same scenario involving lots of food, elegant dresses, presents, and flowers. The practice of casually visiting very close friends uninvited, mentioned earlier, serves, among other things, the purpose of making the occasion more low-key by not allowing the hosts time to cook mounds of food before the guests' arrival.

Men and women at traditional get-togethers often prefer to hang out separately, with women and men sometimes sitting at different halves of long tables. Before the start of a sit-down dinner free-roaming guests tend to cluster around people of their own sex.

SHARING A MEAL

The importance of food in fostering relationships is emphasized in the commonly used expression *chorek kesmek* or "to share a loaf of bread," which implies special ties to a person with whom you've shared a table in the past. People with whom you "share bread" will be more open to handling your inquiries in the future and may approach you with requests of their own.

While traveling, if you find yourself sharing an enclosed space, such as a train compartment, with strangers, it is polite to offer them to join you when eating. Eating in someone's presence without offering to share your food is extremely rude. The invitees are likely to thank you and to decline politely. You can do the same when a similar offer comes your way, unless you want to use the opportunity to strike up a conversation and to sample what's on offer. When you see someone eating or need to interrupt a person who is having a meal, it is polite to start with wishing them *bon appetit* by saying "*Nush Olsun!*"

Chill Averse

Most people in Azerbaijan have a deeply rooted distrust of cold drinks—as well as air-conditioners, fans, and drafts. Cooled juices, water, and milk are feared as inducers of sore throats in summer and winter alike. An American friend, who offered to share a refrigerated bottle of beer with one of her domestic staff, saw the middle-aged Russian woman put her glass of beer in a microwave to heat it to room temperature before taking a sip. So, make sure to ask whether your guests want those ice cubes in their drinks.

FAVORS

If you travel back and forth often, you may be asked to act as a courier in both directions. People frequently ask their foreign-bound friends to take items available only locally between them and their families.

DATING

The ever-changing social norms make dating both a common but also a highly uncomfortable ritual for romantically involved Azerbaijanis. Despite traditional prohibitions, many couples can be seen holding hands on the streets in Baku, and many unofficial relationships flourish underground, away from the public eye. It is not unusual to see young "love birds" kissing in parks and secluded alleys. Even though such behavior may invite an admonition from a casual passerby, it is widely tolerated.

The Azerbaijani language has no word for "dating," just words for engagement and marriage. When a couple is engaged, that allows them to spend a certain amount of (nonsexual) time together before tying the final knot, but the process of becoming engaged implies that a couple must jump through the hoops of parental approval.

There are still many arranged marriages in Azerbaijan. They are particularly prevalent in rural areas, where casual dating is practically impossible.

If you are a woman thinking about dating an Azeri man, his family is likely to disapprove of marriage to a foreigner, for every Azeri mother-in-law wants a compliant Azeri girl joining her household, whose family can be thoroughly investigated through neighbors and relatives before the marriage is given the green light. They won't care as much if the two of you are just having fun and hanging out together, as their boy gains experience with women.

If you are a man planning to date an Azeri woman, she is likely to be interested in marriage only. As we have seen, "dating" does not really exist in Azeri culture, so her going out with you is already a big step toward modernity (or a big sin, depending on whose take it is), let alone being in a loose relationship with an uncertain end. In the worst-case scenario, her male relatives may come after you.

Today, there are many mixed marriages in Baku between Azeris and Westerners, but the absolute majority of those are between Azerbaijani women and men from elsewhere. These marriages are at the center of debates among conservative Azeri males about the falling morals of modern Azeri women.

The prime age for marriage for Azeri women is in the early to mid-twenties. Many women, whose coming of age coincided with the hard post-Soviet years of economic and social upheaval, invested their time in education and careers rather than marriage. As a result, Baku now has a growing number of unmarried professional women in their mid-thirties who won't settle for the traditional lifestyle, and whom most Azeri suitors consider too old for childbearing and too independent to build a family with.

NAMES IN AZERBAIJAN

Azerbaijani first names are varied and come from different backgrounds—some are of Arabic origin, others are Turkish or Persian. Often, ordinary Azeri words, such as "joy," "happiness," "dream," "joke," "enough," or "revenge," can be used as names. In the Soviet days, names such as Marx, Tractor, or Ingilab (Revolution) were sometimes bestowed upon the newborn.

It was not customary to give Russian names to Azeri children, but centuries under Russian rule made it fashionable in Baku to modify Azeri names by adding Russian endings conveying endearment, a trend that is still occasionally followed even among post-Soviet Azeri youth. For example, a person named Rufat may be called "Rufik" by his friends, an Ismail can be become "Issik," an Aytan (a female name) can turn into "Ayka," and a Leyla can sometimes be called "Leilasha."

There are no middle names in Azerbaijan (and there is an official policy of only one name per child) but the Russian tradition of using a father's name after the first name is still in practice. In all official documents, women's and men's names are followed by their father's names with "gizi," which means "daughter of," and "ogli," "son of," respectively.

The question of surnames, the third component of Azeri names, has been at the center of discussions for the last twenty years. Most Azeri surnames end with the Russian endings "-ov" (for men) and "-ova" (for women). Ever since the collapse of the Soviet Union, there has been an ongoing debate about abandoning the newly irrelevant Russian endings.

The matter is further complicated by the fact that some people's last names have the Iranian ending "-zadeh." Pan-Turkists often opt for the Turkish ending "oglu." Some Azerbaijani patriots insist that indigenous Azeri ethnic names should all end with "li," as in "Abbasli" or "Mammadli," or with "soy," as in "Mammadsoy," yet others are convinced that no endings to the last names are needed at all.

In 2010, the parliament was still discussing whether to adopt a law requiring everyone to alter their surnames to officially approved authentic ones. If the law is passed, a massive change of surnames is going to cost dearly—both the economy and the citizens who will have to legalize hosts of official documents bearing their old names.

chapter five

PRIVATE & FAMILY LIFE

FAMILY LIVING

Azerbaijani family networks often include not only the nuclear unit but also numerous in-laws, siblings, cousins, and their offspring, called *gohum-agreba* in colloquial Azeri, derived from the Arabic word *aqareb*, which means "close" and is applied to describe close kin. Relatives on the maternal and the paternal sides have different titles.

Traditional Azerbaijani housing reflects the closeness among extended families. Rural homes may be built as compounds where families belonging to the same clan live close to one another. In Baku, urban living in multistory apartment complexes and the arbitrary manner in which apartments were assigned in Soviet days made this custom hard to follow. However, with the arrival of capitalism, which gave people freedom to buy any apartments that they could afford, many families have gravitated toward the same arrangements. Newlyweds often buy an apartment in the same building as their parents, which comes in handy when grandparents start helping with their newborn babies and young children. Those who cannot afford a separate living space share an

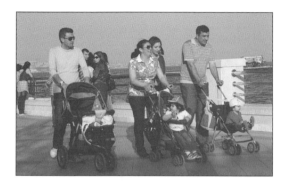

apartment with their parents (in male-dominated
Azerbaijan, it is usually the husband's family),
which often creates domestic tensions.

The relationship between a young bride (*gelin*)
and the mother of her spouse is often strained. The
frequently encountered mistreatment of *gelin* was
highlighted in a popular Soviet-era Azerbaijani film
Gaynana (Mother-in-Law), in which a modern bride
stands up to her mother-in-law's traditional ways of
handling their relationship, often to comical effect.

In addition to taking care of the home, women
also often have full-time or part-time jobs. In some
families, shopping is the man's responsibility, but
in many others, women rush to grocery stores
and vegetable markets after work to stock up on
supplies for cooking a scrumptious evening meal.

HOUSING
In the past decade, the inflow of oil money has
facilitated an unprecedented construction boom in
Baku, with thousands of skyscrapers-in-the-making

towering over everything in sight. Some sites have names such as Yeni Hayat (New Life), suggesting a change from the cramped Soviet living conditions to the spacious apartments with underground garages and newly planted trees. People's attitudes to these new buildings differ from admiration for their

roomy designs (an average apartment in a *novostroyka* is at least twice as big as its Soviet-era alternative) to distrust of their ability to withstand the rattle of a potential earthquake that can strike a fault line in Baku at any time. In November 2000 a 6.2 magnitude quake left many old buildings damaged but not destroyed. The new edifices have not yet been tested in a similar way.

INSIDE AN AZERBAIJANI HOME

Azerbaijanis like to keep their homes clean and well-decorated. Many apartment interiors can be palatial, decorated with lacquered wooden floors, expensive wallpaper, exquisite furniture and carpets, and boasting modern appliances. The women of the house make sure the homes are impeccably clean, either by spending long hours polishing them or by hiring relatively inexpensive domestic help.

Mushrooming furniture stores sell a variety of designs—from the ubiquitous rococo to the "modern" or classic style. Azerbaijani words for many furniture items (as well as the word for furniture itself) are borrowed from Russian. In pre-Russian times, traditional Azerbaijani homes were furnished primarily with carpets, on which people sat for dining and where they spread mattresses and pillows to sleep on at night.

Kitchens are usually modern and equipped at least with a washing machine (usually, there are no dryers, the preferred drying method being a line with clothespins), and, increasingly, with dishwashers and microwaves in the homes of the growing middle class. A gas stove and oven are present in every home with a gas supply.

Bathrooms have floor-to-ceiling tiles and imported toilets and basins. You will also see little hoses with taps fixed near the toilets, intended for use in lieu of toilet paper, which may be absent as many Muslims consider its use an unclean option reserved for non-Muslims.

Summerhouses

Baku's life is deeply connected to beaches and the sea. The sweltering summer heat drives many residents out of the dusty city and into the seaside suburbs, where many own small houses called *bagh* in Azeri and *dacha* in Russian. You are likely to be invited along. Road traffic in Baku in the summer months is much less hectic than in the rest of the year, although it gets extremely congested on the narrow streets of the suburbs leading to the beaches. The most precious part of any *dacha* are the old fig and mulberry trees whose shade offers protection from the unforgiving summer heat.

No dacha experience is complete without *samovar* tea and the marinated lamb grilled (always

by men!) on large skewers over a *mangal*—an old and tired (from decades of use) but highly functional charcoal spit roast. In August, cheap, mouthwatering watermelons, ripe and sweet, are sold by the suburban roadsides.

THE DAILY ROUND

The streets of Baku are nearly deserted before 7:00 a.m., with heavy traffic starting to pick up at around 8:00 a.m. and reaching its peak between 9:00 and 10:00 a.m.

SUMMER FRUIT TREATS

Azerbaijan has abundant fruit in the summer and most women spend long hours making a variety of preserves for the winter. Fruits are carefully cooked in their own juice, with lots of sugar, to help each piece stay intact and to ensure that the end product does not turn into jam. The preserves are served in small saucers with teaspoons, to be eaten as dessert with hot tea.

In addition to the long list of fruits and berries that are usually made into preserves (such as white and black cherries, strawberries, raspberries, blackberries, and quince) Azerbaijani chefs are known for using rose petals, watermelon rind, and baby walnuts (cooked before their shells harden) to make delicious preserves.

Most offices start their working day at 9:00 a.m. and many shops open at 10:00 a.m. and stay open till 8:00 p.m. or later. The lunch hour in most private and government offices is between 1:00 and 2:00, or 2:00 and 3:00 p.m., but Western companies take it at noon, an hour earlier than the regular Azeri lunchtime.

The school day starts at 8:00 a.m. Those public schools that lack the space to house all the enrolled pupils at the same time have two shifts during the day—morning and afternoon.

Shopping for Food

Many residential buildings in Baku have small shops that sell food and basic necessities. For greater variety, residents use the large supermarket chains that have sprung up throughout the city. Their shelves are well stocked with imported products and you are likely to find many familiar-looking foods and even some of the well-known brands. Still, many (especially dairy) products are distinctly local, and you have to try them to know what they are and whether you like them. Expat- (mostly, Indian-) owned grocery stores stock items that are not part of the regular local diet, such as Cheerios and broccoli, or tahini for your homemade hummus.

For chicken, eggs, and dairy products, many Azerbaijanis prefer local stores and street sellers who sell fresh village (*kend*) produce. Milk and yogurt are not pasteurized, chickens are not frozen, and eggs have bright orange yolks with a richer taste than their pale commercial farm equivalents.

Baku's open markets (such as Teze Bazar, best known among expats) have shrunk significantly in size in the past decade, due to the wide availability of fresh produce in small shops and supermarkets. But markets are still good places to look for excellent fresh fruits and vegetables and to bargain. If you arrive early in the morning,

you may be asked by salesmen to buy more or not to bargain too hard, referring to the belief that the first customer of the day (called *sifte*) sets the tone for the rest of the day, including the price and the amount to be sold.

When buying vegetables and fruits at the markets or from street sellers, buyers will ask where the produce comes from (some regions of Azerbaijan are well-known for their delicious fare, while products imported from overseas are often distrusted as containing too many pesticides and being genetically modified). Everything is cooked from scratch; frozen dinners and packaged foods are virtually unknown to most people. Azerbaijanis use grains and legumes, such as basmati rice, barley, buckwheat, chickpeas, and beans in their daily cooking.

Bread is bought fresh daily. It comes in different shapes and types but the most popular, tastiest option is *tendir,* baked in stone ovens and sold steaming hot straight from the mom-and-pop bakeries. At about 50 cents per one-pound (nearly 500-g) loaf of bread, it is an important part of the local diet.

Large Western-style supermarkets sell packaged meat but most local grocery stores also serve as butchers, and many have sheep and cow carcasses hanging from large hooks, from which customers can ask for particular cuts. Livers, hearts, and testicles are also on sale. Street butchers offer heads and hoofs for a local specialty called *khash,* consumed mostly on cold winter early weekend mornings (think 6:00 a.m.) with garlic, vinegar, and vodka, and followed by a long afternoon hibernation.

Fresh pork is not easily available in meat shops. This does not mean, however, that the locals don't eat pork at all. Most people eat a variety of cooked and smoked sausages, as well as bacon-flavored chips or cheese.

PAKHLAVA, THE AZERI BAKLAVA

A special word must be said about the mouthwatering Azerbaijani national delicacy, *pakhlava*, a rich, multilayered, rhombus-shaped dessert made with honey and a variety of nuts. Azerbaijan grows many kinds of nuts (hazelnuts and walnuts are exported) and it imports some more, so there is no shortage of walnuts (*goz*), hazelnuts (*findig*), and almonds (*badam*) to make the delicious treat.

Some shops sell good-quality *pakhlava* in one-pound (nearly 500-g) boxes, which can be brought back as an inexpensive (about US$7) and almost always welcome gift from Azerbaijan (unless the receiver is allergic to nuts or is on a low-carb diet). Be cautious when buying *pakhlava* in regular  grocery stores, where it can be either too dry or too soggy with sugar syrup. A good-quality *pakhlava* has thin, soft layers with a generous filling of well-ground nuts and flavorful honey.

Other Shopping

Clothes and accessories are sold in two categories of stores: shops that sell relatively cheap imported garments, and designer stores that feature price tags well beyond an average person's monthly salary. Both often sell products of questionable quality, although most are marked as having been made in Turkey or in Europe (not necessarily true). Some stores that manage to occupy a niche for the middle class enjoy good business.

Kids' stores, in particular, do very well in a culture obsessed with children. The UK-based Mothercare chain has been opening stores in new locations due to the high demand for its relative balance between quality and price.

Bargaining is acceptable at the open markets and in many shops that sell clothing, except designer stores and franchises. The discounts may or may not be significant but bargaining is almost always expected, though a foreigner haggling for an extra buck may bewilder impoverished street sellers. If you decide to bargain, a leading question is "*Ashagi yeri var?*" (literally "Is there space for a lower price?") Sometimes, the answer is an enthusiastic nod, at others it's a categorical "no," but it may be worth a try. When shopping for touristy items, such as national souvenirs, and especially, carpets, bargaining is almost always expected.

COST OF LIVING

In 2009, Baku jumped to 20th place from 109th in the ECA International's annual "cost-of-living" survey, superseding all other post-Soviet capitals, including Moscow. In 2010, Baku was listed as 31st, behind Moscow but still one of the most expensive cities in the world for expatriates. Prices for utilities and food often reach those of large Western cities. The only category that is still considerably cheaper than in developed countries is the low cost of human services, also called "competitively priced labor" in business manuals. Home cleaners, cooks, nannies, and drivers are paid an average of US$300–500 per month.

GROWING UP IN AZERBAIJAN

Azerbaijanis are very affectionate with children—there are plenty of hugs and kisses for babies and toddlers who are often carried around by loving relatives rather than being allowed to crawl or toddle around, as the streets and floors are generally deemed unclean.

Child mortality is high and feared, and this is likely to be the reason why many babies wear small blue beads, aimed at diverting the "evil eye." Golden pins, chains, or bracelets, with a dangling anti-evil amulet, are

the most appropriate and popular presents for new parents. It is customary to say "*Allah Sahlasin*" or "*Mash'Allah*" when talking about young children, which invites God's blessings to protect the child.

Parenting Styles
Parents and caregivers show love the best way they know how: by being doting and protective and by making sure that their children are well fed, warmly dressed, and kept out of harm's way. Many caretakers in parks and playgrounds are heard cautioning children against running, climbing, and jumping, and otherwise discouraging them from physical activity that can lead to falls and scratches.

People on the streets are usually very friendly with babies and toddlers, initiate play with the

bala, and often attempt to hug and kiss them without their parents' consent. If you don't feel comfortable with such shows of affection by strangers, politely hold your child close to you, but keep in mind that these actions are a well-intentioned attempt to please both the baby and the parent. Also, keep an eye on strangers giving your child candy—it is considered a friendly thing to do and most people give children candy kept in their pockets especially for the purpose.

Complete strangers may also freely dispense advice in relation to how your child is dressed (usually, not warmly enough) and on other aspects of child rearing, particularly to younger-looking and therefore automatically assumed to be inexperienced mothers. Since show of respect to women with age and experience is a must, politely thank the woman who is offering you advice, even if you are not planning on taking it.

Child Care Options
With the number of subsidized state kindergartens declining sharply and the number of unemployed women ready to offer child care services for affordable prices on the rise, nannies are the preferred child care option. When available, female relatives usually help young mothers to raise children. Some parents use the services of the expensive private day care centers that have proliferated in recent years.

EDUCATION IN TIMES OF TRANSITION
Schooling
Once children turn six, they must go to school—a departure from the Soviet practice of starting formal schooling at seven—where they remain till the age of seventeen.

According to a study done by the Open Society Institute, among several post-socialist states surveyed, Azerbaijan had the highest ratio of students using private tutoring, a must for college-minded students, in addition to attending obligatory government schools. This reflects the high value that parents attach to their children's education and the need they feel to provide the best possible opportunity for them to continue education beyond high school.

A slew of expensive private schools has opened in Baku over the past decade. Some are managed by

expatriates, which attracts wealthy Azerbaijanis who believe in the superiority of Western educational standards and in the importance of learning English from native speakers.

Higher Education

All university applicants must take a single national university entrance exam, indicating the subjects they would like to study along with several universities of their choice. The placements are made according to the exam score—those who receive higher scores are accepted into more competitive schools.

There are several higher education institutions in the country, the most prestigious of which are in Baku. It is not always easy to find work after graduation and many diploma-holders accept jobs that are not directly linked to their fields of study.

Received Wisdom

The Soviet education system, while prized for its quality in its day, has left a legacy of rigidly formal relationships between teachers and students. This trend is reinforced by the hierarchical nature of Azerbaijani society.

Visiting Western lecturers to Azerbaijani universities sometimes find it difficult to stimulate a discussion among students, who are not accustomed to questioning the lecturer (which would be considered disrespectful), as opposed to memorizing the dictated lectures. It is uncommon for students to address their teachers by their first name

without adding the respectful "*Muallim*," which means "teacher." University cafeterias have separate sections for teachers and students.

CONSCRIPTION

Azerbaijani men aged eighteen to thirty-five must serve in the army for eighteen months. Reasons to obtain a deferral from compulsory conscription include certain health conditions, disability, and enrollment in institutions of higher education (persons with higher education serve twelve-month terms).

chapter six

TIME OUT

Most modern-day Azerbaijanis are busy holding down one or more jobs to make ends meet and don't have much time left for leisure. In addition to a total of about twenty days off on the country's calendar, Azerbaijan's labor code requires employers to provide twenty-one to thirty days of vacation and to observe a forty-hour working week, but in reality many of the "gray economy" jobs are unregulated. Some people complain that the quantity and quality of their leisure time have dwindled since the collapse of the socialist system.

When Azerbaijanis do have some time off, most of them spend it with their families, visiting each other at home and celebrating special occasions, such as weddings and birthdays, with much gusto in restaurants and the Palaces or Houses of Joy. Socializing is an important part of the Azerbaijani way of life and people of all levels of income find time and the means for parties, which is reflected in the rapid multiplication of restaurants and beauty salons.

Whether held at home or in a restaurant, Azerbaijani parties are warm and jolly affairs involving much toasting, joking, music, and often lively dances. Eating is a central part of any

Azerbaijani gathering and both hosts and guests at any party pay much attention to the food.

EATING OUT
Snacking on the Go

Azerbaijani street stalls, eateries, and chain stores offer a long list of fast-food options that can be consumed on the spot. There is a wide variety of snacks, consisting mostly of baked or fried wheat pies with different fillings, including delightful selections of vegetable and herb stuffings.

The most traditional of these is the half-moon shaped *gutab*, a very thin, round tortilla folded in two and filled with either ground lamb (and, sometimes, sheep tripe) or with greens, such as spinach, leeks, and cilantro (coriander). Meat *gutab* are usually sprinkled with sour, maroon-colored flakes of dry spice called *sumakh* (barberry), to offset the taste of lamb fat. Plain yogurt is also used for the same purpose with dishes rich in fat.

Pirozhki—a Russian dish that has been happily assimilated—is much thicker and smaller than a *gutab* and can be filled with vegetables, legumes, or meats, including beef, potatoes, brown beans, mushrooms, and cabbage. Another ubiquitous snack that has migrated from Russian cuisine is *blinchik*, a Russian crêpe filled with meat or unsalted cheese. A relatively recent addition to the list of popular baked snacks is a Georgian *khachapuri*, a square-shaped envelope of phyllo dough stuffed with salty cheese. *Lahmajun* is a thin Turkish pizza with ground lamb that comes in regular or spicy (*aji*) varieties; it is quickly baked in an oven after you place the order.

Another quick hot snack is the ubiquitous *doner kebab*. A grill attendant will cut small pieces of greasy meat (almost always lamb but occasionally chicken) from a slowly turning vertical skewer, put them in a roll or on thin *lavash* bread, add some veggies, mayo, and ketchup, and you are all set, in less than ten minutes. *Doner* shops are generously sprinkled throughout the city. They also usually sell *ayran*, a popular Azeri drink made of yogurt and water.

Fast-Food Joints

If you want to be served a quick hot snack by a dexterous waiter, you may consider Turkish-style fast-food cafés, such as the Anadolu chain, where you can select from a variety of salads, one or two soups, and several entrées on display, usually stews and barbecues. McDonald's is also very popular among the young.

Azerbaijani Cuisine

Some of the best-known Azerbaijani dishes are *plov* (long-grain, saffron-flavored, buttered rice that can be served with a variety of meat, dry fruit, and bean garnishes), *dushbere* (thumbnail-sized lamb dumplings floating in rich broth spiced with vinegar), *dovga* (a yogurt soup made with spinach and other types of greens), *dolma* (grape leaves stuffed with ground lamb), and a long list of others.

One of the local specialties is the Caspian sturgeon, accompanied by a tiny pitcher of *narsharab*, a sour-sweet pomegranate sauce, to be poured on to the fish.

Most of the Azerbaijani dishes are regional specialties. Many originate from Lankaran in the south of the country (such as *levengi*, fish or chicken stuffed with walnuts and plum spices),

and from the northwestern region of Sheki, with its mutton specialty of *piti* (a rich stew cooked in individual clay pots).

culture smart! **azerbaijan**

DOLMA

The word "dolma" in Turkish and in Azeri means "stuffed." Almost any type of vegetable can be made into a *dolma*,  including the most popular vine and cabbage leaves, bell peppers, tomatoes, and eggplants. Unlike its Mediterranean equivalent, Azeri *dolma* is always a main course dish, stuffed with fatty meat and served with garlic-enriched yogurt on the side for improved digestion.

Local Restaurants

Azerbaijanis are rightfully proud of their rich national cuisine, but you won't be able to sample it in most cafés and restaurants, which offer little more than a range of barbecued and fried meats and mayonnaise salads. A few places, however, serve many of the popular national dishes at affordable prices, such as a chain called Sheki or the popular restaurant Beh-Beh.

Many local restaurants have borrowed from neighboring Turkey the custom of bringing you a tray with a wide assortment of meze-style cold starters to choose from: usually, salads, fruit, and pickles. Be careful, though: if you don't make your selection, you may end up with the tray's entire contents moving on to your table and you will be charged for it later.

Some local eateries do not have menus in English (some do not have menus at all, leaving it to the waiters to recite the list of available dishes) and many will not bring an itemized bill at the end of your meal, unless you ask for it. As a result, you often don't know how much you will finally have to pay, and the cost of the same selections may vary from one visit to the next, depending on the manager's mood or on the way they assess your financial situation. If you look like a foreigner, you may be overcharged.

TIPPING

There is no tipping culture, in Western terms, in most of the country, although the practice is starting to make an appearance in businesses in the capital exposed to Western influence. Sometimes a grateful patron may round up a bill by a few dollars, but this is certainly not expected in most restaurants, beauty salons, or by other service providers, including taxi drivers. However, underpaid workmen providing services in your home on behalf of large companies expect a gratuity of at least US$10.

Small facilitating payments are widely accepted for smoothing minor transactions. A restaurant bill always includes taxes, so you are expected to pay just what is stated on the bill—which may sometimes be only a waiter's scribble on a piece of paper, or even just a verbal statement.

International Restaurants

Baku has a large number of international restaurants, including Indian, Thai, Italian, Brazilian, Chinese, Spanish, French, Ukrainian, Russian, and Georgian, among others. Most of the international cuisine is located in the downtown area. Many establishments serve reasonably good imported wine. The more upscale joints accept major credit cards. Tipping (at about 10 percent) is expected in the Westernized restaurants but not added to the bill.

A CASH SOCIETY

Keep in mind that, with the exception of hotels, supermarket chains catering to expats, and international restaurants, almost no shops accept credit cards. ATMs are most plentiful in downtown Baku but also exist in the city's outlying districts. All have Azeri, Russian, or English menu options, dispense US dollars and Azeri manats, and have an upper limit of 250 Azeri manats per withdrawal.

Currency exchanges are ubiquitous throughout Baku and will readily exchange US dollars, euros, Russian rubles, and UK pounds sterling. A few major banks will accept travelers' checks.

Teahouses

Strong, hot, unsweetened tea is *the* drink in Azerbaijan. It is regularly consumed, even in the middle of a sweltering summer day, when a pot of freshly brewed black tea is believed to make one feel cooler. The traditional pear-shaped glass for tea, called an *armudi*, is a national symbol, often sold in souvenir shops.

Traditional *chaikhanas* (teahouses) are mainly a male domain but some in the city center have started catering to a growing female clientele. Teahouses are popular stopping spots on the highways that cross the country. They usually serve tea spiced with thyme (*keklik otu*), accompanied by a variety of delicious fruit preserves (*murabba*).

The tea is brewed in small round pots. The darkness of the drink in a glass is regulated by adding different proportions of tea and water. Usually, the brewed tea is strong enough to require only about a quarter of the glass to be filled with it; the rest is hot water. Iced tea is not popular, and virtually unknown to people who have not been exposed to Western cultural influences.

Coffee Shops
Until recently, Baku had almost no coffeehouses, and it is still hard to find a good cup of coffee anywhere in the city, where the standard fare is a cup of Nescafé instant. One of a few notable alternatives is the Baku Roasting Company, a coffee shop that roasts, grinds, brews, and sells its own brand of coffee

(also available in half-pound, 250-g bags, for around US$10).

Cold Drinks

When pomegranates are in season, freshly squeezed pomegranate juice is a must-try. Some restaurants serve this rich-tasting, burgundy-colored drink in pitchers. Don't confuse it with the pomegranate juice sold in packaged boxes, which is much more watery than the freshly squeezed option.

You can also ask for *kompot*—some restaurants may serve it. This home-style drink is made from a variety of fruit boiled with sugar. A local specialty made with *shipovnik* or *itburnu* (rosehip) is also a pleasant drink, rich in vitamin C.

Alcoholic Drinks

Alcohol is readily available in Azerbaijani restaurants and supermarkets. Vodka is the typical men's drink that accompanies casual dinners and meetings to discuss business over *kebab* and adds to the fun at weddings and birthday parties.

Until recently, wine making and wine drinking have not been part of the local tradition. Wine is rarely drunk with everyday dinners at home, without a celebratory purpose. Most people don't have a deep knowledge of wine products, and many casual wine drinkers are women who prefer it sweet. Rich and flavorful dry wines are rare and costly imports. Local wines, such as Giz Galasi and Yeddi Gozel, are drinkable. The local champagne, XXI Esr, is a cheap, cheerful, sweet,

and fizzy drink that is typically drunk at New
Year's celebrations on December 31.

Beer has been popular, mainly among men, for
decades, and local breweries make the drinkable
Khirdalan lager. A couple of new small pubs
brewing their own beer have popped up in town.

> ### FORTHCOMING ATTRACTION
> Not yet on the shelves or the menus, a new
> drink is about to start being manufactured
> in Azerbaijan—a liqueur made with walnut
> husks. With equipment imported from
> Germany and ethanol imported from
> Ukraine, it is intended for export.

AZERBAIJANIS ON VACATION
Traveling to the Regions
Many Azerbaijanis travel regularly to the regions,
especially in the summer. Whether you are
visiting for a few days only or for a longer stretch
of time, it is well worth a trip. The landscape
changes magnificently and the quality of air
improves greatly as soon as you reach the hills and
forests away from the dust and bustle of Baku.

It takes at least two hours by car to get from
Baku to the closest woody destinations of
Shamakhi and Pirgulu. The furthest from Baku
are the forested mountains at the northwestern
borders with Georgia and Russia, which can be
reached after six to eight hours of driving. These

most beautiful destinations are great options for a long weekend.

Vacationing in Azerbaijan's mountainous resorts is still expensive, given the quality of service. Nevertheless, most hotels are fully booked on summer weekends and reservations are recommended. Young Azerbaijanis and their expat friends also frequent the picnic spots and hiking trails of the Azerbaijani countryside, sometimes assisted by tour guides. There are only a few companies offering such services, but their number is growing.

Traveling outside Azerbaijan
People who can afford the rising air fare prefer vacationing outside Azerbaijan. Some of the most popular summer destinations are Antalya and Bodrum on Turkey's Mediterranean coast, especially for families with children (chartered flights make this option cheaper than comparable deals inside Azerbaijan); young people prefer exploring Istanbul and European cities; the older generation may head for the Russian mineral resorts of Yessentuki and Kislovodsk.

Going to the Beach
For most Azerbaijanis, however, travel outside their country remains firmly out of reach. In the summer, Bakuvians ride in cars and buses to beaches where fun is cheap and joy is abundant.

Even though during the day the Absheron sands are just as hot as the streets of Baku, the pleasant sea breeze and diving into the warm

waters of the Caspian make all the difference.
Many locals and some of the more adventurous
expats continue to swim in the Caspian, despite
the annual warnings issued by the government
that the presence of harmful bacteria makes it
unsafe. They grill themselves on the sand and
conventional wisdom has it that walking barefoot
and burying oneself in sand has many healing
qualities.

IN BAKU

The rapidly developing capital of a state fueled
by petrodollars, Baku has something to offer to a
variety of tastes, even though many of the newly
available options seem to be catering to the small
group of its moneyed elite and to its sizable
expatriate community.

Outdoor amenities in the city are limited to
a few parks and squares with newly installed
fountains and to open-air restaurants. There are

also tourist attractions within a short drive, such as: the Gobustan petroglyphs—included in the list of the UNESCO World Heritage Sites as "bearing testimony to 40,000 years of rock art"—which feature carvings of animals, boats, and dancing people; the Mud Volcanoes, filled with cold, bubbly mud that can be ignited by  the strike of a match; the eighteenth-century fire worshippers' temple called Ateshgah; and the "burning mountain" of Yanardag, which has been continuously in flames for the past fifty years.

Parks and Walking
Locals and expats alike love going for walks in Baku's historic Old City, exploring its narrow, crooked streets, climbing the tall spiral stairs of  the centuries-old Maiden's Tower, and entering the low doorways of the palatial quarters used by the Shahs of Shirvan in the fifteenth century. A popular Baku summer pastime is also hanging out in parks. The government has been investing some of the oil dollars into developing parks throughout Baku, no easy task given its desert climate. With the exception of tall,

aging poplars and acacias in a few old parks and
the ubiquitous pines planted decades ago
throughout the city, the greenery is usually
limited to palms and trimmed shrubs that are
pleasing to the eye but do not provide much
shelter from the heat. Hence, parks start filling
up with people late in the evenings, usually after
8:00 p.m., and stay full till way past midnight
(children's usual bedtime is much later than
in the West).

Several parks have a variety of fun rides,
carousels, and swings, as well as battery-operated
plastic cars and the increasingly popular
bouncers and trampolines. Playgrounds that
encourage simple physical activity—with sand,
slides, and climbing poles—are still a rarity.

The best-known and most-used park in Baku
is the hundred-year-old, seaside Bulvar. Nearly
two and a half miles (4 km) long, it is a place of
many attractions for children and adults,
including colorful "musical fountains," a newly-
built 3D cinema, and an old 98-feet- (30-m)-tall
observation wheel known as the "Devil's Ring."

One of Baku's largest and greenest parks, the
Botanical Garden, is hidden away from public
view, near the Badamdar district. Behind the
inconspicuous gate that lets visitors in between
8:00 a.m. and 8:00 p.m. is a large area containing
tall old trees, many of them fragrant cypresses.

The current Zoo, located near the Ganjlik
metro, has ancient facilities and cramped quarters
barely suitable for the bears, lions, tigers, leopards,
and elks found on its premises, but it will be
demolished soon and replaced with a new large
Conservation Park outside Baku.

Sports and Gyms
Azerbaijanis are big football (soccer) fans, eagerly
following the World Cup and the European
Championship on TV. Many have favorite teams,
mostly among the European clubs, and all are
very emotional about the Azerbaijan national
team, which has not yet qualified for either of the
above, despite being coached by invited stars of

international football. Azerbaijan also has several football clubs with multicultural teams. One of them, owned by the son of a wealthy state minister, signed a three-year contract in 2010 with Tony Adams, a former Arsenal defender, to coach the team for three years. Boys in every courtyard kick balls around, dreaming of football fame.

Except for the facilities in international hotels, there are few gyms to speak of and men don't exercise regularly. Jogging is not very popular, partly because of the unsuitability of most Baku streets for pedestrian traffic. The few dilapidated stadiums open to the public seem to attract mainly men, although occasionally one may see a couple of jogging women. Instead, women prefer doing aerobics and participating in shaping classes in "women-only" clubs.

Women's Getaways

Many women in Baku spend a great deal of time on their appearance. Most take care of their hair and nails daily and would not consider going outside without putting on some makeup. High heels are always in fashion, and many young women squeeze into some very tight pants.

Beauty salons are often combined with spas and offer a range of services from facials and relaxing massage to aerobics and swimming lessons. Belly-dancing classes and aqua aerobics are also very popular. These clubs are the exclusive domains of women and almost all of them feature large signs prohibiting male entry. This way, women can be assured that this precious time, allotted to caring for their bodies while relaxing by chatting with other women and smoking an occasional cigarette, can be enjoyed uninterrupted by unwanted male attention. Women on the sauna benches cover their bodies with rejuvenating oils and share stories about their daily concerns, romantic troubles, and family obligations.

Men's Hangouts
During off-work hours (and for some unemployed men, this means all day long), many men hang out in the yards and parks playing table games such as dominoes, backgammon, or chess. Many sit in the ubiquitous *chaikhana* teahouses, sipping tea, smoking, and chatting. These activities are almost never shared by women, who

congregate on benches in the yards keeping an eye on their children and sharing community gossip.

Smoking

Smoking is ubiquitous among men and, increasingly, among women. For women smoking in public is a major act of defiance, but it is common in private settings. Nonsmoking restaurants and cafés are still a novelty, limited to touristy places in the city center. However, in 2010, the parliament was discussing a new law that would prohibit smoking in public places.

Music

Several music halls across Baku often host concerts by local and visiting rock stars. The State Philharmonic Hall and the State Conservatory regularly hold classical concerts, as does the Kapellhaus, an old German church turned into a cultural center. The Opera and Ballet Theater is very popular among locals and expats.

Traditional music includes performaces by
ashugs (itinerant singers) and folk ensembles
playing string instruments such as the *tar,
kamancha, ud,* and *saz;* wind instruments such
as the *zurna* (clarinet) and *balaban* (flute); and
the drums *nagara* and *gosha-nagara.*

The deeply spiritual *mugham,* or *mugam,*
traditional folk music, has a special place in the
Azerbaijani heart. The International Mugam
Center was built in late 2008.

Baku's urban heyday in the 1970s saw a rise in the number of improvising jazz performers, one of whom, Vagif Mustafa Zadeh, founded a unique music style called *jazz-mugham,* which combines Western and traditional oriental techniques. Mustafa Zadeh's daughter, Aziza, is a renowned pianist and composer living in Germany. Contemporary jazz can be heard in the Baku Jazz Center and in the smaller but more intimate Baku Jazz Club. For the past few years, Baku has been hosting the International Jazz Festival, keeping up with its former image of "jazz capital of the USSR."

Art

Baku's noteworthy art community is clustered in and around buildings assigned for decades as studios by the government. There are several galleries throughout town that host regular exhibitions of local artists' works.

Paintings from Azerbaijan have made their way into many private collections around the world. The desperate 1990s, when artists had to part with their creations for next to nothing, have given way to world-level prices, a process facilitated in part by international art investors.

Museums

The most notable new addition to Baku's museum scene is the Museum of Modern Arts, designed by the French architect Jean Nouvel and facilitated by a former Guggenheim Museum director, Thomas Krens. The museum has more than eight hundred works of modern Azerbaijani artists, and is definitely worth a visit.

The more traditional Museum of Fine Arts, as well as Azerbaijan's History Museum, a beautiful Museum of Literature, a centrally located Museum of Carpets, and a unique museum of miniature books in the Old City, are among other rewarding places to visit when exploring Baku.

Theater and Film

There is little on offer for English-speaking theater and film lovers in Baku, but if you speak Russian or Azeri you may enjoy exploring the existing options.

The Russian Drama Theater has plays in Russian for adults and children. Occasionally, visiting troupes from Russia cause tickets to be sold out weeks in advance, but otherwise most plays do not attract full houses. The Azerbaijani Drama Theater, as well as the Theater of Musical Comedy and the Theater of the Young Spectator, stage colorful productions in Azeri. There is also the Puppet Theater, centrally located at the Bulevard. The newer, small theaters Yug  and Ibrus are popular with intellectuals. Ibrus also shows feature films and documentaries.

Baku's largest cinema, the "Azerbaijan," is centrally located at Fountain Square. It usually screens a mix of thrillers and romantic comedies dubbed into Azeri and Russian, which attract Baku's young. The most recent movie theater to open is the Park Cinema, in the newly constructed Park Bulvar mall.

chapter seven

TRAVEL, HEALTH, & SAFETY

Azerbaijan has been investing its oil revenues in significant infrastructure improvements. Over the past few years, existing roads across the country have undergone a major upgrade, new ones have been built, and Baku has gained several large bridges and highway junctions that have helped to ease the city's congested traffic. The new bridges have the year of their completion proudly displayed, perhaps to remind future generations of the times of abundance that allowed for such large-scale projects. Nevertheless, a lot of decaying Soviet infrastructure remains, although, surprisingly, some of it is relatively well-maintained.

If you are the kind of traveler who relies on clear street signs and detailed road maps, you will be frequently frustrated. If, however, you come without a detailed schedule or expectations of predictability, you will find Azerbaijan a charming place to explore, with many wonderful surprises along the way.

The public transportation system, despite being quite old and sometimes confusing, is extensive. In Baku, the metro is the cheapest and the most popular way of getting around, followed by buses and taxis. In the rural areas, buses and trusted Russian Niva cars climb up to high mountainous villages and hurry back along winding country roads. Some of the shabby old buses departing on long journeys to the country's regions are prone to occasional breakdowns en route, with passengers having to flag down another bus going in the same direction.

Whether you are riding a bus in Baku or in the villages, you are likely to become a center of attention—after all, not too many foreigners ride public transportation—and may have fellow travelers wishing to share their stories and to hear yours. You will also see many local passengers chatting with persons sitting next to them. On longer journeys, they may offer to share fruit or snacks with you: on airplane rides, vodka shots often pass around between neighboring male passengers befriending one another.

ARRIVAL

All visitors traveling by air land at the Heydar Aliyev international airport (GYD). Keep in mind that there is no elevator between the section where you arrive on the second floor and the ground floor, where you collect your luggage. You have to go down two flights of marble stairs with carry-on luggage and children before joining the hustling lines for the passport control booths.

Be prepared to see people who have arrived later than you trying to jump ahead, as well as important-looking airport staff taking their acquaintances'

passports straight to the immigration officers'
booths without them standing in line. For domestic
air travel, a different airport building is used, the
refurbished old Baku airport of the Soviet days.

Travelers should note that they can no longer
receive an Azerbaijani visa at the airport. Following
a new regulation in 2010, with a few exceptions,
they have to apply for a visa prior to their trip at an
Azerbaijani embassy.

GETTING AROUND BAKU
Metro
Baku has a reasonably efficient subway system

that can get you a
cross town quickly,
especially when cars
remain motionless in
traffic on congested
city roads. It has a
total of twenty-two
stations positioned
along two main metro
lines. The longest ride takes about fifty minutes.

To get onto the platform, you need to buy an
access card for about US$2 and then charge it with
a desired amount. Each ride costs about 15 cents.
You have to buy the card even if you only intend
to use it once. However, each card can be used
multiple times at each station, so you and you
companions can use the same card to get in.

Most of the stations are located deep under the
ground and some escalator rides take a few

minutes. Beware that escalators move very fast, which makes most locals reluctant to walk up and down the moving stairs. In 2005, one person

died and several were injured in a tragic escalator incident at one of the deepest central stations.

Baku's *metropoliten* sports many wonderfully decorated stations, featuring large, shiny chandeliers and impressive examples of monumental art on the walls. The Nizami Ganjavi station is adorned with exquisite colorful mosaics based on themes from the writer's best-known poems.

Buses

There is an extensive network of buses crisscrossing the city. Even though there are assigned stops (often near metro stations), buses stop every time someone flags them down or when someone inside asks to be let out by shouting "*Sakhla!*" (Stop!) to the driver. If you know exactly which bus you need and where to get on and off, they are a good, inexpensive way of traveling. Passengers pay the driver, or his assistant, when they get off the bus. When the vehicle is crowded, people pass coins and bills to the driver through others; any change will make its way back by passing through the hands of the other passengers.

People may sit and stand, filling every inch of a small vehicle, and you may be asked to hold someone's heavy bag on your lap if they are standing. It is uncommon for anyone to refuse such a request. If you are the one standing with a heavy bag, a person sitting in front of you may attempt to take it from you and place it on their lap out of courtesy. Thank the person politely and decline the offer if you are uncomfortable with this arrangement, but be prepared for them to insist. It is customary to offer one's seat to women, the elderly, and people with young children.

Taxis
Unless you are driving yourself, the best way to reach your destination is by taxi. There are many private taxis in town, ranging from decrepit Ladas

 to luxurious-looking old Mercedes, which can be flagged down on the streets. Many of them have a magnetic yellow light placed on the roof, which is often removed after the passenger gets into the car. This is not necessarily a cause for alarm; most drivers are just trying to avoid being fined by the police if they are caught operating without a license. The unregulated nature of the taxi business means that there are so many self-styled cars for

hire that they make little profit at the end of the day and don't want to share any of it with the authorities. A typical ride within city limits will cost you between 5 and 10 manats (roughly, US$6–12), a steep increase from the US$1–2 that used to cover almost any ride prior to the gasoline price hike of 2006. There are no meters in any type of taxis.

Usually, any driver will be happy to oblige if you offer to hire him for the day or longer. Negotiate the price in advance, taking into account the working hours and the distances to be driven.

Walking and Biking
Baku is not a very pedestrian-friendly city, mostly because of the lack of pedestrian areas free from either parked or speeding vehicles.

The same applies to cyclists, although, with the exception of the mainly expat Baku Bicycle Club, there aren't too many bikers crossing town. It takes some courage to navigate the streets of Baku on a bike because of the unruly traffic and the city's hilly landscape, strong winds, and extreme temperatures in summer and winter. Besides, most local males would view themselves on a bike as uncool and most women would be labeled immodest.

Driving
You can rent a car in Baku from Avis or Hertz, or from one of the few recently established local companies. The price (around US$75 a day) includes insurance and unlimited mileage. For an additional US$50, you can hire a driver to work for you between 9:00 a.m. and 6:00 p.m. You need to

present a valid passport, a driver's license, and a credit card.

Driving may turn into quite an adventure if you don't know the city well and aren't used to pushing your way through a crowd of aggressive motorists. If you end up driving anyway, take reasonable precautions, do not automatically assume that other drivers will respect your right of way, and keep in mind several local variations of the rules.

Unlike what you may be used to, when an approaching car repeatedly flashes lights at a pedestrian or at another driver waiting for his or her turn at a traffic circle or a crossroad, it does not mean "You can go, I will slow down." It means exactly the opposite: "I am warning you that I am coming." One courteous blink, however, is likely to signal to a driver waiting for a chance to turn that they are being given the right of way.

On highways, when many cars in the opposite lane seem to be flashing their lights at you for no obvious reason, it means that, in an act of driverly comradeship, you are being warned that there is a traffic police car hidden around the corner, waiting for your speeding vehicle. It may also mean that other drivers are warning you about something they've noticed wrong with your car, such as a flat tire or a door or trunk inadvertently left open.

The system of traffic lights may create confusion too. As elsewhere, green, yellow, and red indicate that it's time to either move or stop. However, unlike many other places where yellow is meant to warn cars that are already at an intersection to move on before the traffic light turns red, in

Azerbaijan you are not allowed to move when the yellow light is on, and drivers who move on yellow are fined. To warn you that the prohibitive yellow is about to come on, the green light will flash briefly. As a result, some drivers, including those who approach traffic lights at full speed, will hit the brakes when they see the first blink of a flashing green. Beware of this if you are driving behind.

Parking

Parking throughout downtown Baku is problematic. The number of signs forbidding parking is growing disproportionately to the number of assigned parking spaces, and they are often ignored by drivers, who park right under the signs.

Illegally parked cars are often towed away. Towing is enforced randomly, however, and some busy downtown streets are notorious for having cars towed within minutes of being left unsupervised by the owners. If you find your car missing upon return, don't look for signs telling you where to find it or where to call. Ask around—perhaps someone on the spot will know—or approach a traffic police car (white and blue, marked "YPX") and inquire about your car's potential whereabouts.

Most available parking spaces have semiofficial attendants wearing green vests, who look after the cars and regulate their arrival and departure, often by standing in the middle of narrow streets to stop the slow-moving traffic so as to allow leaving cars to back out into the road (waiting for such a courtesy from other drivers would take a long time). Departing drivers pay 20 gepik (about 20 cents) to the attendants regardless of whether their car was parked for minutes or hours. In the busiest, most sought-after parking places, attendants may charge more: from 40 gepik to 1 manat (about a dollar).

TRAVEL OUTSIDE BAKU
By Car
Azerbaijan is a small country that can be crossed by car from its northwestern border with Russia to its southern border with Iran in less than a day—though it would be a long day if you attempted it! The government, eager to promote internal tourism, has greatly improved all major roads. The infrastructure is slowly following suit, with mushrooming new hotels and restaurants.

The system of highway signs has improved compared to the Soviet days, but still leaves much to be desired. Signs directing drivers to the most popular destinations are prominent, but otherwise you may have to rely on a good map and intuition. If planning to drive at night, keep in mind that roads outside Baku are poorly lit and may have potholes or standing vehicles without flashing warning lights.

There are four national highways leading out of Baku. The city has two main exits. A new outer ring road connects the two main arteries, the M1 and M2, to help cross-country traffic go around the city without entering its busy streets.

The southern exit road starts beyond the large Bibi Heybat Mosque and the Shikhov beach. It becomes the M2, which turns west and, via an uninspiring arid steppe for much of the way, leads to the city of Ganja and to the former jewel of Azerbaijani tourism, the Goy Gol Lake, now inaccessible to tourists because of its proximity to the occupied territories. The M3 road branches off from the M2 and continues down south to Lenkeran, and to picturesque places such as Lerik.

The northern city gate lets through traffic onto the M1 road heading north to the magnificent forests of Guba and to Azerbaijan's famous mountain village of Khinalig, which is an hour's drive from the woods and beaches of Nabran.

The same road also handles vehicles going northwest. This route has most to offer to tourists. The M4 separates from the M1 going to Guba soon after you leave the city limits. It leads to the old Azerbaijani capital of Shamakhi (including side trips to Lahij, with its famed silver jewelry, and to Pirgulu, which houses an old Soviet sun observatory). A scenic road (40) will bring

you from Shamakhi into the beautiful canopy of the Ismayilli woods, and then on to the scenic town of Gabala, which has a couple of good hotels and a new luxurious resort that hosts an annual international music festival in the summer (Gabala is also home to a Russian radar station).

From there, it's a short drive to Azerbaijan's most interesting historic city of Sheki, which has the fifteenth-century Khans' Palace with stained glass windows (*shebeke*), a caravanserai turned into a cozy hotel, mosques, a fortress, and some five-hundred-year-old trees. Make sure to visit the village of Kish to see a crumbling, ancient Albanian church. Further up the mountains lie the wonderful hiking

destinations of Gakh and Ilisu, and then you get to the border with Georgia and Russia.

By Bus
Most destinations are served by a regular bus service to and from Baku. A new large international bus terminal (that also has a Comfort Inn hotel) is well equipped to handle thousands of passengers departing for and arriving from villages around the country daily.

Riding these buses to the regions is safe and crime free, keeping in mind the usual dangers of Azerbaijan's unruly road traffic; some bus drivers, confident of their knowledge of the frequently traveled roads and eager to make up time, may take unnecessary risks. If you are an unaccompanied woman, engaging in conversation with strange men may be misinterpreted as an invitation to remain friends for the rest of the trip.

By Train
To purchase a train ticket from Baku's central railway station you need to show your passport. You also need it to board the train.

There are two types of train departing from Baku railway station: with and without sleeping berths. The cars with rows of wooden seats are called *elektrichka* and they make frequent stops at most Azerbaijani towns. The same towns can also be reached on trains with sleeping compartments that go to Georgia and Russia.

The compartments that have four sleepers (two on top and two at the bottom) are called *kupe* (koo-peh). Tickets for cars with only two berths (called SV / pronounced "es-veh"/ which stands for "special vagon," that is, a more upscale car in Russian) cost twice as much as for the *kupe*. Tickets are sold to passengers without consideration of gender. If you are unhappy with a companion, you can ask the attendant (*provodnik*) to help you switch compartments with someone for a small extra fee. Be prepared to handle similar requests, especially if you are riding alone in a two-sleeper. Some solo travelers buy two SV tickets to keep the entire compartment to themselves and to have some privacy. Train attendants will be persistent in asking you to give up your vacant berth(s), as they are trying to sell them to passengers who are traveling without tickets and making arrangements on the spot.

Generally, the attendants are in full control of the situation in the cars and run them as their own small enterprises. They are in charge of the distribution of clean bed linen and hot water for your tea or instant coffee, and they expect to be paid for it, usually a fixed price that is the same for everyone. If they see you as a paying customer, you will be treated with the utmost respect and friendliness. They also knock on doors in the morning, about an hour before arrival, to wake up passengers who may still be sleeping.

HEALTH

Back in Soviet times, health care in Azerbaijan was free and available to all, and many people still have the firm belief that government-provided health services are a basic human entitlement and that doctors charging high fees are corrupt and immoral. The Azerbaijani government followed suit by declaring all state-owned medical facilities and their personnel to be at the service of the people for no charge. The reality, however, is still far from that intent. Many doctors are underpaid and make up the difference by accepting, and sometimes charging, extra payments from patients.

The quality of care tends to be substandard, even in facilities that have been upgraded and supplied with modern equipment. For illnesses that require serious attention, all expats, and many locals who can afford it, travel to other countries. The most popular destinations for diagnosis and treatment are Moscow, Tehran, and Istanbul, but also Germany and Israel.

If you end up visiting a local doctor, even with a common cold, you are likely to be given a long list of prescribed drugs. Doctors' skills are often judged by the ease with which they can juggle a variety of Latin drug names. You may also be prescribed herbs, which are a popular treatment option. Most pharmacies sell a variety of herbal mixtures along with conventional medication.

Pharmacies
Make sure to bring with you a stock of generic drugs for cold, fever, allergies, and upset stomach. Local pharmacies may or may not have the brand you are used to, and some of their products may be counterfeit and ineffective.

Immunizations and Common Diseases
The local immunization schedule for children is similar to that in Western countries, with the exception of a tuberculosis vaccine, which is given

to all newborn babies in the first days of life. TB is a serious problem in Azerbaijan. Spread mainly through former inmates, it is endemic in prisons and is the number one killer of the incarcerated. Another widespread disease is hepatitis B, which sometimes gets passed on through reused needles at hospitals. If you decide to get a manicure or pedicure while in Baku, do check how well they sterilize their equipment.

Think twice about swimming in the Caspian in the summer, as there are frequent occurrences of *E. coli* in the water from sewage that gets dumped into the sea.

Drinking Water
The water in Baku comes from the Kura River and it is known for its poor quality. It is not safe to

drink tap water and most people boil it or use bottled water. Tap water samples have also occasionally shown the presence of *E. coli* and other bacteria.

SAFETY
Crime
With a population of three million, Baku is considerably safer than many cities of its size around the world, owing in part to tight police control and in part to its idealistic Soviet past. Until just a few years ago, many people did not lock the doors of their apartments and some still leave their cars unlocked. Even though car theft does happen, it is not common for cars to be broken into if something, such as a purse or a laptop, is left on a seat.

Violent crimes involving foreigners are rare, but make sure not to stay out too late and avoid poorly lit areas outside the city center at night. In the event of something being stolen from you, it is not always worth the time spent jumping through bureaucratic hoops to file a police report. The chances of their finding the perpetrator of a small theft are minimal.

Sexual Harassment
Walking long distances is almost always unpleasant for women, who are likely to be harassed by men driving and walking past. Intimidating stares are the least that you should be prepared to handle. Dress down if you don't want unwelcome attention.

Traffic

The most treacherous part of living in Baku is undoubtedly the road traffic. Neither drivers nor pedestrians follow the traffic rules, resulting in many deadly accidents. The majority of drivers are unaware of pedestrians' right of way. Only a few traffic lights have countdown timers for pedestrians, and most don't have a pedestrian light at all.

Aggressive driving is the norm, and most drivers act on hunches, sizing up one another for a second before deciding to brake or to speed off. The din of honking horns is ceaseless and is often added to by personalized audio signals, such as sirens and animal howls.

Reckless bus drivers, often tired from working very long hours in a highly stressful environment, are well aware that the size and decrepit condition of their vehicles gives them a clear advantage over smaller, fancier cars, and barge ahead without paying much attention to others.

Other Natural and Man-Made Hazards

The sidewalks of Baku's poorly lit streets often have open manholes and stairs leading down to basements.

Strong winds sometimes escalate into powerful storms that can force down trees and street poles and cause heavy objects to fall off tall buildings and construction sites. So, walking and parking close to them can be hazardous.

If you are in Baku in the summer, take precautions against the heat and exposure to direct sunlight. July and August can be brutal, so make sure you stay well hydrated, have sunscreen with you, and, when temperatures soar to over 104°F (40°C), avoid going outside in the afternoon heat.

In the winter, beware of the days following heavy snowfalls. The few hours when the city stands white and beautiful are usually followed by an icy mess, including slippery sidewalks, which are rarely cleaned up, and dangerous roads. If you are driving behind an old Lada struggling up a slippery hill, it may end up sliding into your car.

Travel Security

Although travel to the regions of Azerbaijan is generally safe, the areas near the line of contact with the Armenian-occupied regions are an exception. They are heavily guarded by the military and prone to frequent exchanges of fire between the warring sides.

chapter eight

BUSINESS BRIEFING

THE ECONOMY

Azerbaijan has risen from the poverty of the past decade, though this is less evident in the rural areas outside Baku. While much of the oil wealth stays at the top and in the very thin layer of the Azerbaijani middle class, it has also been trickling down to the rest of the population.

Gone are the early post-Soviet days of cheap labor, and it is a lot easier to find work—the construction, business, and service sectors provide a large number of new jobs—even though wages are still low compared to those in the West. With a few well-positioned top-managerial exceptions, most people are continuously searching for better paid jobs, either inside or outside Azerbaijan. Many official salaries are significantly lower than actual earnings, and a large part of the economy remains off the books.

Oil

The proceeds from oil and gas comprise about 60 percent of Azerbaijan's GDP. In 2010, the Fitch's Azerbaijan Country Ceiling was raised due to "the rapid increase and prudent management of oil revenues that are being used to build a strong public and external net creditor position."

The oil proceeds are invested in a sovereign wealth fund: the State Oil Fund of Azerbaijan Republic (SOFAZ), established in 1999. Its assets, regularly updated at the Fund's Web site, reached US$22 billion in the middle of 2010.

Inflation and Economic Crisis

Inflation grew steadily over the last decade, reaching more than 20 percent in 2008—a sign of the economy's overheating from the inflow of cash—and fell dramatically in 2009  to 1.5 percent due to the fall in international commodity prices.

Azerbaijan dealt reasonably well with the global economic crisis that started in 2008, mostly due to the limited exposure of the private sector to international financial structures. In 2009, the government cut some expenses and achieved GDP growth of 9.3 percent, ensuring an encouraging pat on the back from the International Monetary Fund, which praised Azerbaijan's prudent fiscal policy in the crisis years.

Diversification

It is estimated that the country's oil reserves will be exhausted in less than two decades, with oil production starting to decrease slowly in 2014. Overreliance on oil could easily turn a prosperous state into a pauper, and there is much talk about diversifying Azerbaijan's economy and inviting investments in the non-oil sector, but little has been done so far to seriously change the situation.

Many major Azerbaijani corporations remain in state hands. However, most of the small- and medium-sized enterprises, as well as agricultural lands, have been privatized, and some have turned into successful international partnerships, including agricultural ventures exporting food products such as nuts and pomegranate juice.

The government is also making a major push to turn Azerbaijan into a tourist destination, borrowing from the experience of oil-rich Gulf states such as Dubai.

The Ease of Doing Business

If you are considering doing business in Azerbaijan, there is encouraging news from the World Bank's Doing Business 2010 report, which

ranks the country at 38 out of 138 states, using such parameters as the time, cost, and number of procedures to start a business. All of these have been halved in Azerbaijan since 2008. The World Bank press release says that "Azerbaijan led the world as the top reformer in 2007/08, with improvements on seven out of 10 indicators of regulatory reform [that] moved it far up the ranks, from 97 to 33 in the overall ease of doing business."

However, the development of Azerbaijan's non-oil sector remains a challenge, requiring significant structural reforms, including battling corruption and improving the business climate and legal framework. The Fitch Rating Report regards the Azerbaijani banking system as weak, despite its rapid growth in the past few years, and mentions structural weaknesses in its economic system. Nevertheless, if you are successful in establishing your enterprise, you can expect to reap the benefits.

THE BUSINESS CULTURE

Doing business in Azerbaijan is all about *who* you know. However, once you have secured support through the right connections, it's up to you to show *what* you know and to prove your credibility.

Many spheres of the Azerbaijani economy, such as banking and IT, rely on the know-how and professional skills of qualified experts. They realize that they can no longer use well-connected but incompetent partners. Successful local companies, which offer their professional staff competitive remuneration—nowadays often higher than many Western entities operating in Azerbaijan—will hire only top-notch talent to run their operations.

SETTING UP A MEETING

Most decisions are made at short notice and if you try to schedule your meeting months or even weeks in advance, you may run into last-minute changes and cancellations or, sometimes, your counterpart may forget about your planned visit altogether, which will cause embarrassment to both of you. Make sure to call a few days in advance and double-check that your meeting is still on the agenda.

Writing versus Calling

If you send an e-mail message to a person who does not know you, don't be surprised if you don't hear back. An old-fashioned phone call still goes a long way in Azerbaijan, and meeting in person is the best communication mode of all.

Personal Recommendation

If you have someone whom you can ask to introduce you, do not forgo the opportunity. It will save you much time and effort, and will ensure that the person you are trying to meet will give you their full attention because they will feel responsible to the acquaintance or friend who made the introduction. Remember that it comes with the mediator's shared responsibility for the quality of your product, so make sure to give him or her full information.

On the other hand, the mediator's reputation plays a big role in how your counterpart will perceive you, so select your partners wisely. Also, be prepared for the person you are trying to meet to assume that the introducing party has something to gain from making the introduction, which is very often the case.

Go to the Top

Just as in politics, the nature of business enterprises in Azerbaijan is largely dependent on the character of the owner. Most successful businesses are managed by persons who established them in the early post-Soviet years or later, and they remain afloat for as long as they are owned by the same individual. Many Azeri business owners prefer to work with their close relatives—the most common partnership is one that involves two or more brothers.

Regular employees are rarely given a chance to contribute to making important decisions; generally they are expected to follow decisions made at the top. Hence your best bet is always to meet with the boss. If you secure a meeting with a mid-level manager, make sure to ask him or her to introduce you to the person in charge in the future.

Dress Code

Dress conservatively if you want to be taken seriously. Azerbaijani dress style is very formal, even in everyday life, and business meetings are always attended in power suits. You will be assessed not only by the cleanliness of your outfit but also by the brand of your watch, the make of your shirt, and the estimated cost of your shoes and suit. Casual, understated dress is not yet common among Azerbaijani government officials and businessmen.

MEETING AND GREETING
Waiting

When you arrive for a meeting, you may be asked to wait. Sometimes, this can be attributed to the

Azerbaijani attitude to time: your host may be discussing something of importance with the previous visitor and is taking extra time to finish off all the details (always considered more important than sticking to the clock). He will be equally prepared to let his meeting with you run longer than scheduled if you have not finished your discussion, and make his next visitor wait. Occasionally, however, this may be a way of conveying to the visitor the host's extra importance. If you can help it, schedule no more than two meetings in a day, spaced well apart, to be most effective.

At the Meeting
At the meeting, use the formal Mr. and Mrs. to address your host. After the initial introductions, you can add local flavor by addressing them in Azeri (see page 153–4).

Respect for elders is important, but business culture has been changing rapidly in the past two decades and nowadays it is not uncommon for an older person to rise when a more powerful younger person enters the room and otherwise show deference and respect. In ordinary social situations, however, it is still important for younger people to let the oldest person in the room speak first and without interruptions and to sit down only after they have done so.

Print your cards in Azeri and make sure that your title is also "culturally translated," so that it is meaningful to your counterparts. For example, the word "officer" does not have any other meaning in Azeri except military, and should not be translated literally; use words such as "administrator" or "manager" instead.

Hire an interpreter who is well versed in both the Azeri and Russian languages.

Keeping a Distance

When you arrive for a meeting, you may be served hot tea in small *armudi* glasses, accompanied by thinly sliced lemon and sugar cubes. Don't be surprised if there are no teaspoons, as the sugar is intended for being placed between the teeth and sucked while sipping tea. Whether or not you are served tea may signal the importance that your host attaches to the meeting.

Exchanging pleasantries is common but should be kept to a minimum at the time of your first meeting. Otherwise, you may be sending a signal to your host that you are not valuing his time and are underestimating his importance. Azerbaijani culture is characterized by high power distance and it is of the utmost importance that you keep an appropriate distance and do not get too personal too early. If you are invited to subsequent meetings, you will have a chance to engage in less fomal talk.

PRESENTATIONS

Make sure you make frequent eye contact with the person in charge. Not looking your host in the eye is likely to be perceived as insincerity. However, if you are a woman, you may find your male partners averting their gaze, especially if they are from a conservative background. There are some

Azerbaijani women in leading positions in business and government, but society still views them as an exception rather than a norm. If you are a female, be prepared to work harder to be taken seriously and to prove the credibility of the business you represent. The more conservatively dressed you are the better.

Presentation Style
Since most decisions are made at the top, large group presentations are unusual. Your meeting is likely to involve only the person in charge and his immediate aides. In the unlikely event that the rest of the team are present, they will leave all questioning to the boss. If they are silent, it may also mean that you either sound too abstract and they don't trust you, and/or that they don't understand what you are referring to and are embarrassed to ask.

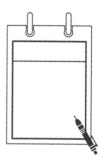

Extensive audiovisual aids are not valued and may be regarded as irritating and time-wasting. Your counterpart may be very busy and have a short attention span, so be sure to summarize your proposal. Also, keep in mind that some businessmen are sensitive about what they perceive as Western condescension. Trying to spell out the basics is often counterproductive, as it signals your desire to educate them.

The person in charge may ask you to submit further details to a subordinate. This may indicate that he is not interested in your proposal. If, however, they ask specific questions, delving into the parts of your presentation they deem concrete and relevant, and if they give other clues that they are interested, delegating the discussion of further details to an assistant is common practice.

NEGOTIATING

Azerbaijanis are inveterate bargainers. They assume that the price you are asking for your product or service is significantly higher than you are expecting to get, so their initial offer is likely to be somewhere between 20 and 50 percent lower than what they are prepared to pay. They may let you leave without agreeing on the final price; they are prepared to resume later. "No" is not usually the final answer.

BUSINESS MEALS

If you are successful in convincing your Azerbaijani counterparts that you are a potential business partner and if they want to get to know you better and to establish mutual trust, you may be invited to a restaurant.

This is a good time to follow your host's lead to become less formal. If they are spicing up the conversation with jokes and personal stories, you can share tidbits of information about your hobbies or interests, especially those that can be easily placed in a local context.

If you would like to reciprocate by treating them to lunch or dinner, make sure not to use phrases such as "I will buy you lunch/dinner." If translated verbatim, it may sound very condescending in the local context. "I would like to invite you to lunch/dinner" sounds much more gracious to the local ear.

CONTRACTS AND FULFILLMENT

Contracts can be highly detailed and bureaucratic, but despite the respect accorded to official company seals and letterheads (called *blank* in both Azeri and Russian), the greatest weight in any agreement is the informal understanding based on trust. The way people respect and fear their business partners plays a far more important role than the amount of fine print in the contract.

Stay in regular touch and follow up frequently. Don't assume that things will move on their own by the deadline indicated in the contract.

BUSINESS GIFTS

The exchange of gifts on the occasion of holidays between established business partners is widely practiced. They help maintain relationships between key management figures. To be valued, gifts must be expensive and must have practical use. Bottles of whiskey and large baskets of nuts and delicacies are common, as are vintage pens and designer ties.

INDIRECTNESS IN BUSINESS

Just as in other spheres of life, the Azerbaijani business communication style is indirect. Saying "no" directly to your face is never easy for an Azerbaijani, who will use his imagination to get his or her point across without hurting anyone's feelings. This is often misunderstood by visitors, who take the words of Azerbaijani officials at face value.

While you cannot definitively judge whether your meeting went well by your hosts' behavior, it is usually a good sign if they are concrete about the timing of the next meeting or any potential future steps they would like to take. Vague definitions, no matter how flattering and flowery, and indefinite projections into the future, such as "thank you for your most interesting presentation; we are most obliged," "call us sometime," or "we will talk/meet again at some point" probably mean that you will not hear from them again and there will be many valid excuses (usually, overseas travel) for why they cannot meet with you when you make an attempt in the future.

Usually, any criticism is passed on through the grapevine. Keep this in mind if you end up working with Azeri partners and staff in the future. Never criticize them in front of the group; it will be perceived as a personal insult and humiliation, no matter how constructive you believe your criticism to be. Instead, use trusted intermediaries to get your point across or find time and space for a private meeting.

chapter nine

COMMUNICATING

CHOOSING YOUR LANGUAGE

As we have seen, language is a sensitive
issue in Azerbaijan. Numerous alphabet
changes, generations of uncertain
status within the Persian Empire, and
significant Russian influence impeded
the development of a modern written
Azeri tradition, leading to determined attempts
to reestablish the legitimacy of the Azerbaijani
language in the two decades following the Soviet
demise.

Many Azerbaijanis express their support for a
return to the country's roots through the conscious
use of their native tongue. Azeri is the main
language of communication in Azerbaijan, but
Russian may still be used in business circles and
socially, even though its influence and spread are
diminishing every year, especially among the
young.

Greetings

The most commonly used Azeri word for "hello"
is "*salam.*" Greetings are usually warm and
expressive. Men joining a group of people in a
room, such as a classroom or a restaurant, greet

each of the men present with a handshake and often a kiss in the air next to the cheek. Women usually kiss each other on the cheek.

No Sex in the City

Reading shop signs and menus in Azerbaijani has become easier for Western visitors since the final switch from the Cyrillic to the Latin alphabet in 2002, but sometimes the similarity of letters can lead to confusion. If, while exploring Baku, you come across signs containing the words *sex* or *sexi* (such as *motor sexi*, for example), don't jump to conclusions. The Azeri word "*sex*" is pronounced "seh" and means a "small factory," the same as in Russian, from which it is borrowed. Small factories producing everything from furniture to home decorations are sprinkled throughout the city and have the *SEX* signs above them.

Addressing People

When addressing a woman, use her first name followed by the respectful *Khanim*. For a man, attach either *Muallim* or *Bey* to the first name. For example, if a man's name is Ali Valiyev, it is appropriate to call him "Ali *Muallim*" or "Ali *Bey*." If a woman is called Leyla Valiyeva, you should call her "Leyla *Khanim*."

Khanim initially meant a woman of a high social status, but with time it has become more widespread. Another word used by Azerbaijanis to address women of their mothers' age is *Khala*, which means "auntie," but this is never used in official situations or toward persons of higher social status.

Polite forms of address to men are somewhat harder to navigate because they have changed with each political regime. The respectful Turkic term *Bey*, used in pre-Soviet Azerbaijan of the early twentieth century, was dismissed by the Soviets for its class connotation (*bey* initially meant a landowner). It was replaced by *Muallim* ("teacher") or the ubiquitous and gender-free *yoldash*, which meant "comrade" and was used throughout the Soviet Union to address both men and women.

When communism went out of fashion in the early 1990s, men searched for a new form of address. *Bey* has made a return in some, mostly nationalist and Turkophile, circles but it has not gained widespread currency. The term *Canab* (pronounced Jah-nab) is the official form of address for men, but you won't hear it on the streets among ordinary people talking with one another. *Muallim*, added to the first name, is still used by most people to address men in a respectful way. Occasionally, a stranger on a street can be addressed as *Vetendash*, but it does have an official undertone since it translates as "citizen."

Singular or Plural?

Similar to Russian, which uses singular and plural forms of "you" to address people of different status, Azerbaijani has the words *sen* and *siz* to serve the same purpose. Common folk, especially in rural areas, often use the singular in all circumstances, but it is polite to use the plural form of pronouns and verbs with people you don't know well, and especially with persons older than you.

So, if you want to ask a close friend how he or she is doing, you will use the singular, "*Sen nejesen?*" and with an older colleague you will use "*Siz nejesiniz?*" To be on the safe side, use plural in most situations.

NONVERBAL COMMUNICATION

Azerbaijanis are very skilled in sensing what is not being said through a complex mixture of signals, such as gestures, eye contact, and tone of voice. They may pay less attention to the content of your speech than to nonverbal clues, including the context of your relationship and your status.

Body Language

Compared to most Westerners, Azerbaijanis need less personal space, both socially and physically. They feel quite comfortable standing very close to one another while talking, gesticulate energetically, and may often touch each other's arms, slap one another on the shoulders, and use other forms of physical contact to make their point. Standing too far from the person you're speaking to signals emotional distance. Most people of the same gender also maintain close eye contact: averting one's eyes is perceived as a sign of insincerity (however, men and women, especially strangers, are discouraged from looking each other in the eye).

If two people are standing close to each other and one accidentally steps on the other's toes, he or she will promptly shake or touch the other's hand.

FREQUENTLY USED GESTURES

- Rubbing the thumb against the index finger means "money."
- Slapping one's lap or knee while shaking one's head means an extreme level of indignation at someone else's behavior. However, the same gesture can also be used by someone who is laughing hard to emphasize the impact that the humorous situation has had on them.
- Wagging a finger at children means giving them a warning.
- "No" is often conveyed by making a "tsk" sound with one's tongue.
- Moving the index finger across the throat means "I've had it!"
- Many men laugh heartily, often with an emphatic slap of one palm on the other, but for women loud laughter is often considered inappropriate. Men and women may also extend an upturned hand to someone in a gesture similar to the American "Give me five!" This means a shared understanding of an understated joke.
- Winking with one eye to warn about a practical joke in the making is widespread.

HUMOR

Azerbaijanis have a long-standing tradition of using satire to mock authoritarian rulers, to address social ills, or to prod someone about matters that need to be brought to their attention without causing too much confrontation.

At the dawn of the twentieth century, Azerbaijani intellectuals published a number of satirical journals that highlighted important social issues of their time.

The most prominent of these was the *Molla Nasreddin* magazine, named after the legendary character, famous throughout the Orient, whose humorous philosophical musings about life's truths are well-known to many Azerbaijanis. The magazine was founded and published by the writer Jalil Mammadkulizadeh, whose satirical stories about the confrontation of modern life with backward tradition are still as relevant today as they were more than one hundred years ago.

A Molla Nasreddin Joke

Once, Molla was riding his donkey past a restaurant. He stopped for a few minutes to inhale the smell of the food, which he could not afford. Seeing this, the restaurant owner approached him and demanded to be paid for the smell, upon which the witty Molla took a couple of coins from his pocket and rattled them near the owner's ear, saying, "The sound of my money is the payment for the smell of your food."

There is a very popular modern form of musical art in Azerbaijan called *meyhana*. This is a kind of rhythmic rap, in which the performer improvises short verses on the spot addressing various aspects of life and lampooning famous events and people.

In everyday conversations, Azerbaijanis often use humor to make a point, but, if you are trying to tell a joke or attempting to grasp what a group of locals is laughing about, keep in mind that humor rarely translates well.

THE MEDIA

There is a large degree of state control over the traditional media, particularly over TV and radio, from which the absolute majority of the population gets its news. None of the existing local stations is free from government pressure and international broadcasters, including the BBC and the Voice of America, were removed from the FM airwaves in 2006.

Those who want to watch foreign channels can do so via cable TV or individual satellite dishes. Hundreds of thousands of them on roofs and windows have their round faces turned either to Europe or to Asia, according to the owners' cultural preferences.

The printed media are divided into pro-government and pro-opposition, with only a few newspapers maintaining a degree of balance. The relative liberty of the press is explained by its limited distribution: even the most popular dailies have circulations of around 9,000 copies, which for a country of 9 million people is 0.1 percent. The best-selling newspaper in the country is the sensationalist Azeri-language *Yeni Musavat*, which belongs to the Musavat opposition party. The most respected and balanced Russian-language dailies are *Echo* and *Zerkalo*, read mostly by the country's Russian-speaking establishment. The combination of a limited market and the expense and infrequency of flights to Baku means that you won't find international printed media on the newsstands, only the free local English-language newspapers.

English-language translations of the news are provided by leading news agencies, such as APA, Trend, Turan, today.az, and the state-owned official Azertaj. These are available on their Web sites, although some won't allow you to access the content unless you are a subscriber.

As the Internet becomes more available to the general population, it is also increasingly being used for political purposes. New online media critical of the government have appeared in the last few years, with a growing following among educated youth. News dissemination via the Internet is growing in popularity, but the government has also started curtailing the activity of independent bloggers.

SERVICES
Telephone
There are virtually no pay phones in Baku or the regions as almost everyone in Azerbaijan has a cell phone (the number of users proportionate to

population has long been one of the highest among the post-Soviet states). Instead of pay phones, you can find cell phones for rent by the minute near metro stations. People who find themselves stranded without a phone can also ask strangers on the street for permission to use their phone; they will be very likely to oblige.

Until recently, there were only two cell phone providers in Azerbaijan: Azercell (which seems to ensure reception in the remotest parts of the country) and Bakcell, which has recently started an aggressive re-branding campaign. Nar Mobile (Azerfon/Vodafone) is a third provider that entered the market in 2007 and is the only one so far that offers 3G mobile Internet access.

There is a great variety of cell phones in Azerbaijan, and they are sold unlocked. Cheap used models for in-country use can cost as little as US$30. Seasoned expats buy the more expensive quad-band GSM models that can be used anywhere in the world with a local SIM card.

To start operating a phone, you need to buy a SIM card (about US$5), often sold in the same shops that sell the phones, and insert it into your telephone. You do need some form of ID to make the purchase. Most cards come with a minimal balance that you can use for an initial call but then you will need to buy more time, called *kontur* and branded *sim-sim* for Azercell and *cin* for Bakcell. Most sellers of the *kontur* cards will be happy to help you upload your credit by punching the digits from the card into your phone, although some cards may have instructions in English. A US$3 *kontur* card buys about 10 minutes of talking time. All incoming calls are free.

If the cell phone you brought from home is of the GSM variety (which is the case for most countries around the world, but not for most US phones), all you need to do is insert an Azeri SIM card into your own phone (however, you do need at least a tri-band phone, which can use the 900Mhz GSM frequency band) to be able to use it in Azerbaijan.

If you are in the country long enough to need a landline (your apartment or hotel room is likely to have one anyway), you can buy one either from the government providers (called ATS, or automatic telephone stations) or from a private provider called CATEL. The landline calls within Baku and local calls within other cities are free.

Internet
If you have a landline, you can either buy a card for (a very slow) dial-up Internet access or hook up the ADSL through one of the numerous companies that offer this service (UNINET is one of the oldest private providers, and Bakinternet is the government-owned option). Azerbaijan's fiber-optic options are out of reach for anyone except large businesses and limited to just a couple of providers, such as AzStarNet.

According to the International Communication Union, there were 3.7 million Internet users in Azerbaijan in 2010, or 44.4 percent of the population (up from around 0.1 percent a decade ago and from less than 10 percent in 2007). Internet cafés are widespread and popular among the young. The Internet is not censored (although, occasionally, some sites have been reported to be blocked by the government).

Mail

The Azerbaijani state postal system has made a huge leap forward in the past decade, from almost complete unreliability to a reasonable rate of delivery of letters and parcels. It takes an average of two to three weeks for both incoming and outgoing mail to reach its destination.

Major shipping companies—FedEx, UPS, and DHL—have offices in Baku. Another alternative to the state postal services is a small private company called PX-Post, which accepts outgoing mail from anyone and delivers incoming mail for its subscribers through their hubs in London and New York. Though expensive (but still cheaper than the private international shipping options listed above), this service is particularly useful for online shoppers buying from stores that do not deliver to Azerbaijan.

Keep in mind, however, that local Customs open *all* incoming packages, leaving parcels and boxes slashed open in the middle and then taped over with duct tape. Nothing better to remind you that Big Brother is watching.

CONCLUSION

If you are reading this guide, you may already be on your way to Azerbaijan. You won't regret it. Whether you have been lured by the promise of the exotic mixture of East and West, or by the blend of steel-and-glass modernity with the antiquity of the medieval Shirvanshahs' Palace and the mysterious Maiden's Tower in the center of Baku, you are bound to enjoy your journey.

You will find a country where, despite the hardships of daily life, people have preserved their ability to be generous and empathic, where long-standing traditions merge harmoniously with the ultramodern, where family and friends make sure that you are never left to feel lonely, and where you will always find a sympathetic ear when you need one.

Even if you don't like everything that you see, you will acquaint yourself with a fascinating region, full of contradictions and rich in history, meet people who will make you feel welcome, and experience a genuine warmth and curiosity that is so often lacking in other places.

Azerbaijan's rich cultural heritage, music, and fine arts will leave you deeply moved and will take you beyond the clichés proliferating in the international media that focus mainly on its oil reserves and politics. You will come to appreciate the eclectic mix of European and Asian influences that make Baku and its people so fascinating.

The flavor of freshly brewed black tea, which will remind you of Iran, mixes with the aromas of strong Turkish coffee; delicious vapors of lamb stew blend with the scent of imported smoked sausages on the table; the sound of Russian disco music blasting from car windows competes with the latest Western hits and with authentic Azeri jazz emanating from others; and the Muslim call to prayer from the numerous minarets chimes in with the ringing bells of a Russian Orthodox church.

Approach this remarkable country with an open mind and let your heart guide you through your excursions, bearing witness to the ups and downs of life of ordinary Azerbaijanis. You will be rewarded many times over.

Further Reading

Altstadt, Audrey L. *The Azerbaijani Turks: Power and Identity Under Russian Rule.* Stanford: Hoover Institution Press, 1992.

Blair, Betty. "The Business of Literature: Who Wrote Azerbaijan's Most Famous Novel: Ali and Nino? Chamanzaminli, Essad Bey, Robakidze, or Ehrenfels." *Azerbaijan International*, Vol. 15.2–4 (2010).

De Waal, Thomas. *Black Garden: Armenia and Azerbaijan Through Peace and War.* New York: New York University Press, 2004.

De Waal, Thomas. *The Caucasus: An Introduction.* USA: Oxford University Press, 2010.

Elliott, Mark. *Azerbaijan with Excursions to Georgia.* London: Trailblazer Publications, 2010.

Goltz, Thomas. *Azerbaijan Diary: A Rogue Reporter's Adventures in an Oil-Rich, War-Torn, Post-Soviet Republic.* New York: M.E. Sharpe, 1998.

Heyat, Farideh. *Azeri Women in Transition: Women in Soviet and Post-Soviet Azerbaijan.* London and New York: RoutledgeCurzon, 2002.

Reiss, Tom. *The Orientalist: Solving the Mystery of a Strange and Dangerous Life.* New York: Random House, 2006.

Said, Kurban. *Ali and Nino: A Love Story.* New York: Anchor Books, 2000.

Swietochowski, Tadeusz. *Russian Azerbaijan, 1905–1920: The Shaping of a National Identity in a Muslim Community.* Cambridge: Cambridge University Press, 2004.

Online
www.azer.com
Azerbaijan International Magazine, the world's largest Web site about Azerbaijan.

Index

culture smart! azerbaijan

Acknowledgment

This book is dedicated to my family—Rauf and Clara.